Urban
Etiquette

Discard

Urban Etiquette

Marvelous Manners
for the Modern Metropolis:

*A Commonsense Guide
to Courteous Living*

By Charles Purdy

WILDCAT CANYON PRESS

AN IMPRINT OF COUNCIL OAK BOOKS ~ TULSA/SAN FRANCISCO

Wildcat Canyon Press, an imprint of
Council Oak Books, Tulsa, OK 74104

08 .07 06 05 04   5 4 3 2 1

Book design by Margaret Copeland
Cover design by Idea Studio
Author photo by Stephen Rahn

ISBN 1-885171-82-X

Author's Note

Social Grace's question-and-answer columns appear in this book courtesy of the *SF Weekly* (www.sfweekly.com). Some material was adapted from Social Grace advice originally published by *Genre* magazine. Where necessary, letters to Social Grace have been altered in a minor way, to ensure the advice seekers' anonymity. Any similarity between a situation described in this book and an actual situation is therefore coincidental. Names used in this book's examples are the product of the author's imagination and are not meant to represent any real person.

Contents

Acknowledgements

can think of no better way to begin an etiquette book than by writing a thank-you note. Of course my debt of gratitude is far too large to be contained by this page, but I would like to try to thank a few of the people who made this book possible.

I am eternally grateful to Elsa Hurley—my agent and friend—for her guidance, patience, and wisdom, and to the Candice Fuhrman Literary Agency. Thank you, Elsa.

I humbly acknowledge the contributions of the good people at Wildcat Canyon Press and Council Oak Books—I must thank my brilliant editor Tamara Traeder, Council Oak's Ja-lene Clark, Sally Dennison and many others who worked on the book. I am also grateful to Robert Ordoña and Rynn Lemieux for their invaluable editorial assistance (and their priceless friendship). Thank you to Karen Zuercher and Deborah Lewis, who edit my *SF Weekly* column (and do a consistently excellent job of it); to everyone at the *SF Weekly* for their years of support; to Laurel Wellman, formerly of the *SF Weekly*; and to Morris Weissinger and Bryan Buss, both formerly of *Genre* magazine. I am grateful to Dave Morey, Renee Richardson, Peter Finch, and Greg McQuaid of KFOG Radio's *Morning Show* for their faultless hospitality (and for choosing my theme song); to Neil Dickens of WTD Public Relations for his hard work on my behalf; to *Macworld* magazine's editorial staff; to my countless exquisitely polite friends and relations; and to my beloved Michael Godfrey.

Thank you, thank you, thank you.

I dedicate this book to the world's courteous strangers—the people who are polite and kind, even to people they do not know, and even when they perhaps need not be. Each day, at least one of you affirms my faith in humanity.

Why Do Manners Matter?

Nothing more rapidly inclines a person to go into a monastery than reading a book on etiquette.

When a new acquaintance asks me how I earn my living, I often hesitate before answering. I'm tempted to say "narcotics dealer" or "gigolo by day, contract killer by night"—because I believe that most people would prefer to find themselves talking with a professional criminal than with *an etiquette expert.*

The very word *etiquette* reminds listeners of a dour, persnickety, unyieldingly ill-humored elderly relative. Most of us don't even have such a relative, but this caricature persists. It may be some kind of genetic memory. I call this largely apocryphal figure "Great Aunt Vivian." (If you happen to be a Great Aunt Vivian, I sincerely beg your pardon.) She represents our instinctual dislike of being told what to do and our secret fears of being found socially inadequate. Grumpy Aunt Vivian makes us feel that everything we do is somehow incorrect. She scowls when a nephew introduces her to a man instead of vice versa, or when he spoons his soup inward. Her eagle eyes never fail to spy improper wording on a wedding invitation, or cut-

1

lery laid across a plate at an incorrect angle. When I tell nice people that I write about etiquette, I can see from their faces that I am metamorphosing into Great Aunt Vivian before their very eyes: I have brought etiquette to a perfectly pleasant cocktail party. I am there to stop the fun; impose meaningless, archaic rules; and worst of all, to *strongly disapprove.*

But I would like you to forget about Great Aunt Vivian's misrepresentation of etiquette (although the dear lady does have her uses as a disciplinarian, and she knows many things we would be wise to keep in mind). Let's leave her to her sugary sherry and her often incorrect interpretation of *etiquette.* In her place, I would like to present a new personification of that word: Mr. Social Grace. (And he would like to say to you, "How do you do.") For several years, Social Grace has been answering etiquette questions in his advice column (which appears in the San Francisco Bay Area's *SF Weekly,* PlanetOut.com, and elsewhere; pieces of past columns are used to illustrate points throughout this book). He has led basic-etiquette workshops for groups ranging from third-graders to financial managers. And he regularly handles the phoned-in etiquette questions of the rock-and-roll fans who listen to the San Francisco Bay Area's KFOG Radio (as a guest of that station's *Morning Show).* Unlike Great Aunt Vivian, and many self-proclaimed etiquette experts, Social Grace wholeheartedly believes in the basic goodness, and good sense, of the average person. The problem is, many of them simply weren't taught how (and why) to behave properly. Social Grace wants to give those people the tools they need in order to let their natural goodwill and courtesy show. He isn't here to beat you about the head and neck with self-righteous disapproval. And he isn't too concerned with teaching you terribly fine etiquette points; for instance, in this book, we won't be discussing how to address the Queen of England. (I can tell you, though, that Her Majesty the Queen *rarely* stops by unexpectedly—you'll have time to prepare before her arrival.) Instead, Social Grace wants to give you etiquette rules that make sense for modern people in a terribly difficult environment: a city.

What Etiquette Is Not

Good manners are widely agreed to be on the decline—this can in large part be blamed on our idea that etiquette is something "unpleasant," "too complicated," and "no fun." After all, who wants to sit up straight and work G-rated jigsaw puzzles with Great Aunt Vivian when we are now free to do anything and everything we choose, without her *tsk-tsking* over our shoulders? We are successful adults! We live in our own apartments in large cities! Of course we want people to be *nice,* but etiquette has nothing to do with that—or so we've come to believe.

The past four decades have seen a major cultural revolution in the United States, and we've made drastic changes in the way we deal with other people. Some of these changes were for the better, but many were for the worse. True, we began to do away with a lot of societal ills—racism, sexism, classism, and so on—but at the same time, we wrongly began

3

to get rid of a lot of good manners, too. They were incorrectly identified as part of the "establishment," or the old, inequitable way of doing things.

The fact that the trappings of etiquette had been misused by certain elitists with bad intentions (who will misuse *anything* given a chance—money, language, power) was unfairly held against etiquette itself. And it is true that plenty of people—many of them are purportedly "experts"—use "etiquette" as a platform from which to look down on others, for reasons that have nothing at all to do with courtesy and good manners. These people are, in fact, snobs. Snobs are the very definition of *rude*. They might have you believe that a well-mannered person must wear this or that brand of clothes, must have attended this or that college, must eat this type of food, or must enjoy opera and speak French, for example. Many people who fear "etiquette" have had it used against them by a snob. Understandably, these people then reject rules of etiquette on the grounds that they are arbitrary, used by a privileged few to keep "certain types of people" in their place. But when someone with an Ivy League education smirks into his martini when you order a light beer or mention that you attended classes at a community college, that person is employing very bad manners, indeed.

What Etiquette Is

Etiquette rules *enforce and communicate* "niceness." True courtesy has always served to make sure that everyone gets his or her societal due—that all people are treated fairly. Social Grace insists that true good manners are available to *everyone*. They are free—that is part of their beauty. They don't require a certain brand name. And etiquette serves to make our dealings with other human beings—all human beings—more pleasant, or at least more bearable. It allows us to work harmoniously with other people (and it leaves them with a positive opinion of us, so they are more likely to work with us again). Etiquette isn't simply about using the correct fork at the correct time—although that is an interesting part of it. Codes of etiquette ease personal interaction and can make awkward situations less so. What's more, etiquette rules are part of our social history; they weave us more firmly into the fabric of society and allow us to assume our rightful places in the glorious tapestry of human civilization.

The good news is, behaving properly is easy, often much easier than being rude. Etiquette can be complex, it's true—and some exclusionary socialites will continue to change the complex rules of the advanced etiquette game in an effort to keep the riffraff from crashing their parties (Many of these parties not much fun at all, believe me—Social Grace occasionally attends them.) But the fundamentals are so easy to master that anyone can play. (If you can learn to operate a car, build a Web page, or assemble a futon, you can learn proper manners—you can even learn to employ them *while* operating a car, building a Web page, or assembling a futon.) As a matter of fact, using the basic points outlined in this book in conjunction with your own common sense, you will be able to move confidently through any situation—and deal confidently *and correctly* with the snootiest of the snooty.

Life in the Big City

Good manners are especially necessary for the modern urbanite. In the past, social rules (which made certain that people behaved respectfully toward the people they saw every day) were easily enforced by close-knit communities and the families within them. If we misbehaved in the small villages of our past, we would soon find ourselves in deep trouble. But in the more anonymous setting of a large city, other people are not as obvious a concern. A person might be tempted to ask questions such as "Why not be curt with this sales clerk I'll probably never see again?" "Why not leave my cell phone's ringer on at the opera?" and "Why not cut off that Toyota with out-of-state plates?" To which Social Grace answers with a smile, "There are some very good reasons."

Living by the rules of good manners can sometimes take a bit of effort. Trust me, I know how tempting it can be to verbally kick people who insist on standing in an escalator's "passing" lane (which is the left side, just for the record). Courtesy can take some willpower. And I understand that its readily apparent benefits—easy communication of respectful treatment, participation in the resplendent pageant of human civilization, and smooth interaction with our fellow humans —are not reasons enough for some people to justify this effort. Occasionally, I am asked, "Why should I bother?" To this question, Social Grace has an answer in three parts:

1. Because you make your community a better place to live.
Simply put, the basic premise of Social Grace's etiquette rules is that when you employ good manners in your daily life—that is, when you are pleasant and respectful to the people around you—you make your community a better place. And why should you care whether your community is a nice place to live? *Because you live there, too.* You benefit. (And behaving properly, even when it is difficult, is good for the soul, the personality, and the complexion.)

2. Because having good manners will get you ahead. We live in an era of individual rights unprecedented in human history: the "Me Generation" has given way to the "ME, ME, ME! Generation." Breaking the "golden rule" is not even a misdemeanor offense any more, no matter how furiously Social Grace endeavors to get stronger punishment for such crimes built into our penal code. *But good manners make other people like you.* And good manners are, unfortunately, uncommon enough that people who employ them stand out from the crowd in a *big* way. Good manners can be a key element in achieving professional success and financial gain—or even in getting dates. If you are continually offending innocent sales clerks, random opera buffs, and out-of-town drivers, you will never find out what they may have to offer you.

3. Because etiquette not only helps you deal with all the other polite people in your city, but also gives you very effective ways to deal with scoundrels. People who are impolite all the time lose out on a powerful societal weapon—I call it "politely applied rudeness." That's right: rules of etiquette have always included powerful ways of dealing with scoundrels, and we will discuss them in later chapters. However, if you already treat all the people you meet as if they were socially untouchable, you cannot use politely applied rudeness. Social Grace's correct methods of censure (from the stern word to the cold shoulder) work best when they are wielded by paragons of politeness. In addition, dealing in the socially correct way with jerks will leave you feeling better (and them feeling worse) than will getting into a knock-down-drag-out shouting match. Those shouting matches—which happen all to easily—leave everyone involved feeling sheepish and unhappy. They keep us up at night, and we need to sleep well. Besides, you're better than that, aren't you?

I have great faith in the power of good manners. And I hope you enjoy reading about some of etiquette's fundamentals and finer points. As you advance in your study of etiquette, remember that the foundation of good manners is respectful concern for your fellow human beings. With that in mind, you will never go too far astray.

So Happy Together

Man is a social animal.

—BENEDICT SPINOZA

As long as people have lived in groups, they have developed languages of social behavior to clarify and simplify communal living. If we don't know or don't employ the local language, we aren't fully participating in society, thereby making it that much less supportable. Worse, not knowing the local language can make our attempts at communication seem childish, incomprehensible, or even insulting. It can prevent us from getting what we want.

I always say that modern urbanites are as prone to iconoclasm as dachshunds are prone to back problems. We like to think that "the rules don't apply to us." But in fact, they do. Etiquette protects individuality (that includes *your* individuality, Bub), which can be hard to stake out in an overcrowded urban environment: It works to ensure that everyone—socialists and socialites, Republicans and rebels, doctors and drag queens—is treated with equal respect and knows how to show that respect for others.

Living with other people, in an urban environment, requires that we accept a few fundamental premises, and that we follow some simple rules:

Some behavior is for the world to see; some is not. As many of us already know (although you may have noticed a few people on your morning commute who need gentle reminders), some behaviors are profoundly private: trimming toenails, flossing teeth, and pleading for forgiveness into a telephone, for example.

All the world *is* a stage, and when we are not at home, alone ("backstage"), we are players upon it. And although our individual parts in the greatest production ever staged may be small, they are important, and we should honor them and our fellow actors. (To thoroughly massacre the theater metaphor, this is your big break—your only chance to be a star in this life).

Apply a simple rule: If you would not want something to be filmed and shown on national television, you should save it for private time. (If you are the sort of person who might appear on a reality-TV show, it may be helpful to imagine what your mother or father wouldn't want you to show on national television.)

Because private activities should not take place in public but, out of necessity, occasionally must, we have mutually agreed to designate some public spaces as "private"; that way, as we make our way through our daily lives, we can take care of such personal matters. Phone booths, public restrooms, and similar areas aren't *really* private; however, we have all agreed to pretend they are, to some extent. One layer of this social pact is the unspoken agreement that when we are in a "private" place, no one else sees or hears our activities (within reason). This is why so many people become uncomfortable when a stranger in a public restroom begins making small talk over a stall wall.

We must also learn to differentiate between what truly infringes on our rights and what merely annoys us. A good portion of Social Grace's mail is from people with questions such as "If a person next to me on the bus is talking on a cell phone, what can I do about it?" or "My sister's new boyfriend has bad breath; how do I tell him?" Here is his answer to such questions: These things are neither your problem nor anything you should seek to do something about.

People can be very annoying, but etiquette is not a tool you can wield in order to make your surroundings suit you perfectly. Yes, there are things you can (and should) do when someone is putting you in danger or willfully being rude to you. But before you look into them, you must make sure that you are not expecting, perhaps, too much in the way of special accommodation. We are trained, as Americans, to highly value individuality. But many people have taken this excellent trait a step too far, mistaking their perfect comfort for an inalienable right. In fact, the health and welfare of our communities—the comfort of the whole group—will sometimes take precedence over one person's comfort. And sometimes, that one person who must deal with some mild discomfort is you.

(I know this may be hard to hear—because sometimes, that one person is me.)

What *Was* that Noise?

Dear Social Grace,

How should one handle someone using a cell phone in a public bathroom? On a recent visit to my company's loo, I encountered a woman who talked on her phone during her entire stay, while those around her did their business. I found it revolting, but I couldn't think of what to say to stop her. Ideas?

Dear Revolted Madam,

And what exactly did you have in mind? "Excuse me, I'm trying to concentrate"? "Pardon me, Miss, but you are sickening me"? Though the average person finds several situations a day in which the latter comment would make sense—and while I agree that using a stall in a crowded ladies' room as a phone booth is a somewhat unsettling misuse of cellular technology—pretty much anything you might have said to terminate her call would have been equally inappropriate. The best advice I can give you would be to ignore others' bathroom behavior, inappropriate and otherwise, as much as you can.

Using a phone is one of those private activities. And yes, there are places cell phones should not be used. But before you interrupt another person's ill-timed call (as you should in some cases—when that phone call is interrupting your enjoyment of a theatrical event, for example), ask yourself this: "Am

I merely annoyed, or is an injustice being committed?" This isn't always an easy question to answer. (A secondary question in this situation might be "Is this person speaking in a place where everyone else is being respectfully quiet?")

People have been talking to one another for thousands and thousands of years, but they have been talking to people outside of physical hearing distance for only a small fraction of that time. Some things can take a long time to adapt to (as evidenced by the large number of people who still feel it necessary to shout into telephones). But it seems that cell phones are here to stay—even Great Aunt Vivian has one. Part of the reason cell phones inspire such strong negative emotions in some people is their incongruity: devices long used only in private are being used, intrusively, in public spaces. Before cell phones came along, public phones were put in booths (and later, in pseudo-booths) for a reason: your phone calls should be a private affair.

When you use your cell phone in public, you should speak in a way that doesn't disturb others. In a restaurant, for example, you should use your phone where your loud conversation won't bother other diners (or insult people at your table): in the area of the restaurant where the public phones are. On public transportation, you should speak in the same voice you would use if you were speaking to someone next to you—and your phone call should be as brief as possible. In movie theaters, symphony halls, and the like, you should turn your phone off.

And consider getting a phone that vibrates—especially if you have chosen one of those very annoying ring sounds that has a tendency to stick unpleasantly in a person's head.

 ## Phone a Friend

Dear
Social Grace,

My best friend constantly pulls her phone out at a restaurant, in the middle of dinner, and right there at the table places a call on her cell phone. Usually these calls are to her boyfriend or to other friends we might be meeting later in the evening, and they don't last long, but they are not emergencies, by any means. I think it's horribly rude of her, because it's basically ignoring me. I've suggested that she not behave that way, but she continues to do it. How should I handle this situation?

Dear Ignored
Madam or Sir,

Well, for heaven's sake. You could tell her again that she is hurting your feelings. You could gently remind her to turn off her phone when you enter a restaurant (by conspicuously turning yours off, for example). You could even show her this letter. Here you go: People who use their cell phones to carry on chitchatty conversations while dining look, to those around them, not only rude but also silly, superficial, and hungry for attention. *For shame.*

If all that doesn't work, there is always politely applied rudeness. Don't allow friends to treat you *too* shabbily. (Or if you do, don't complain about it to advice columnists. Friendship often involves compromises.) The next time she whips out her cell phone, excuse yourself from the table—take a leisurely trip to the restroom or stop by the pay phones to make your own call. Or pay your portion of the check and ask your food server whether you can finish your meal at the bar or take it home. If Chatty Cathy is behaving like a person who needs to be alone—and by your account, that is just what she's doing—then leave her alone.

Incorporate a pleasant "Good morning," "Good afternoon," and "Good evening" into your interactions with the people you speak to throughout the day. It will not only make the people you say it to feel better, but also make you feel better. The benefits of prefacing simple transactions (at a cash register, as you board a bus, or as you join a colleague on an elevator, for example) with one of these handy phrases are immediate and long-lasting. I think you will be amazed at the goodwill they engender (and, indeed, in many other languages and cultures, using only "Hello" to begin a conversation with a shopkeeper, for example, is downright rude). Use "Excuse me" and "Pardon me" liberally as well, whenever you must pass by someone or inadvertently inconvenience someone, even slightly.

Of course, you ought not interrupt a stranger in the midst of doing something else to wish him a cheery good day—don't force contact (even eye contact) on people who obviously don't want to engage you in it.

Good Morning!

**Dear
Social Grace,**

Like many people, I work in an office building and take public transportation to work. After my stop, it's about a two-block walk to work. I am a naturally fast walker and am likely to pass some work acquaintances on my way. Am I supposed to slow my pace to theirs, walk with them the rest of the way to work, and discuss the latest benefit our employer is trying to take away? I usually mutter hello and give a vague wave of my hand; these gestures are probably unheard and unseen. (I'm not too civil in the morning until I've had that first cup of coffee, which I get at work.) I frankly have very little in common with many of these people, other than the fact that we work at the same company. If I were to leave the company, for example, I would never see most of them again unless I ran into them at a mall or something.

Thanks very much for your advice.

**Dear Walking,
Talking Madam
or Sir,**

While we sympathize with your need for morning caffeine, I'm afraid the Social Grace Math Quorum isn't going to let a cup of coffee affect this etiquette equation. If you find yourself absolutely unable to be civil without your morning cup, I suggest that you have it a bit earlier in the day. Etiquette neither asks that you engage every acquaintance or coworker you meet on the street in lengthy conversation nor endorses phony bonhomie with colleagues. But muttering and vague gesturing might give the people at your office a rather negative opinion of your personality, and workplace relationships should at least be pleasant.

More effective than muttering would be some eye contact and a sunny (or as sunny as you can manage pre-java) "Good morning, Ms. Werner. I'll see you at the office" as you stride purposefully by. You won't lose more than a few seconds on your way to the office coffee pot, and you may find that acting pleasantly will improve your mood.

Try to regard each new person you meet as a potential ally or friend, and turn on the charm. What new people have to offer us is not always evident at first.

Shake hands firmly—but not too firmly. Many people follow introductions with an attempt to cause physical pain. (If you can feel that you are pressing your partner's fingers together, your grip is too tight.) A firm handshake can also be gentle, and watch out for people wearing rings: your firm handshake does not leave a good impression if it also leaves a scar.

Some etiquette sticklers would remind you that, outside of business situations, a lady gives a man her hand to shake (a gentleman does not offer his hand first). If you think you might be revolving in such old-fashioned circles, gentlemen, be a bit cautious. And ladies, you can help out here by remembering to offer your hand first (if you are prepared to shake hands, that is), thus pre-empting any uncertainty on a fellow's part. In the main, however, society recognizes such gender differences less and less often, and any refusal to

Soothe the Savage Breast

Well-mannered people try to assume the best—that is, we imagine that when an acquaintance behaves badly, he does so through accident, oversight, or even ignorance. But sometimes these assumptions are difficult to wrap one's mind around. If you find that your attempts in this direction are giving you a headache, try some Chopin (the Nocturnes are a good choice) or some Joao Gilberto, or a bit of vintage Van Halen if that's the music that relaxes you. Wait until you're in a better mood before you decide, for once and for all, that someone you know is a jerk, or before you remove a new friend from all future guest lists.

shake hands will likely startle a new acquaintance.

If you have a condition that prevents comfortable handshaking, a simple explanation can mitigate any hurt feelings: "Forgive me for not shaking your hand, but I have a wrist injury. I'm very glad to meet you." Even something such as "I'm sorry, but my hand is a bit sensitive today" probably won't raise too many eyebrows, what with the modern-day prevalence of repetitive-strain injuries and the like.

It's not easy being irresistible. Many modern people have unique ideas of "hugging etiquette," and people new to this social custom may find a hug too familiar for recent acquaintances. (Note to huggers: Try to restrain yourself when dealing with unfamiliar people.) There will be the occasional person who catches you unaware, but it is difficult to hug someone who has extended her hand for a handshake. So if you prefer not to be grabbed, get your hand into position, smile warmly, and shake, shake, shake. To make that handshake even warmer, use both hands, placing the left on top of your and your new friend's right hands. This movement forms a sort of "hand hug," a friendly compromise well-suited both to reserved folks and to a cuddly metropolis.

There is a proper way to introduce people to one another. You should know this order of precedence, just in case you meet people to whom it matters (they are increasingly few and far between)—people to whom it *doesn't* matter will not even notice the difference. A man *is introduced to* a woman—so say the woman's name first, and then introduce the man ("Maxine Fortnight, may I present my dear friend Roberto Saintly; Roberto, Maxine teaches my yoga class," or "Aunt Jerri, this is my colleague Brad Tangelo; Brad, this is my aunt Mrs. Geraldine Posthaste"), a younger person *is introduced to* someone considerably older ("Mother, this is my friend Maxine Fortnight.") And finally, a regular Joe is introduced to an estimable personage: "Senator Noteworthy, this is my brother-in-law Guy Standard." When you do introduce people, it's a good idea to give both parties full names (so they can properly address each other), and to give them some idea of whom they are talking to (as in the preceding examples).

"How do you do!" We used to have a wonderful phrase in the English language, though we rarely hear it anymore, except in some parts of the United Kingdom and in countries where people have learned English solely from textbooks. That phrase is "How do you do"—an idiom that doesn't mean exactly what it says. Curiously, it isn't even a question. The correct response to "How do you do" is "How do you do"—without even a change in inflection. What it means, basically, is "This is a friendly greeting. I bear you no ill will."

But a generation or so ago, this handy term fell out of favor. It was too square, man! It was what parents and authority figures said! It was hypocritical, even!

The problem is, we threw out this important phrase— before we had a replacement ready. We reached for a close approximation to "How do you do," and came up with "How are you?" as the best alternative. But "How are you?" is still in use as a real question, unlike "How do you do."

I would love to bring back "How do you do"! There is still time; these words are still clinging to life. Barring the widespread return of that exquisite little phrase, you must use your wits and interpret "How are you?" each time it comes up. I know you can do it. For example, when a close friend says over brandy and cigars, "Chris, my dear, how are you?" she means the phrase literally: you are invited to unburden yourself of your cares and worries. When the ticket taker at the corner movie house says, "How are you?" he is employing an idiom that means "This is a friendly greeting." The correct response is "Fine, thank you." These are examples of meaningless social blather used to express goodwill and friendly intentions (depending on how they are said, of course), and as such, they should be responded to with more of the same. It isn't exactly Dorothy Parker, but it will have to do.

When you forget someone's name, admit it. When I run into someone I barely know—whether I remember her name or not—I say something like "I'm Charles Purdy; we met at Vanessa Vanderziel's Easter brunch; I'm Vanessa's coworker." Saying that helps her out if my name has momentarily escaped her (you should never say anything like "You don't remember me, do you?" to a person), and it often prompts a person to answer by saying her own name. (To which you can smilingly answer, "Of course"—whether or not you had the name at the ready.)

If you do forget the name of someone you don't know very well and there will be no avoiding the issue, simply apologize sincerely and try to say something demonstrating that this person stayed in your memory, even if his name did not: "I'm terribly sorry—I remember our fascinating conversation about fractals word for word, but your name escapes me." The rules are the same when making introductions. Rather than attempting "Please, introduce yourselves" (which is both mildly impolite and *completely* transparent) or, worse, not introducing two people who should meet each other, you'll just have to apologize for your momentarily nonfunctioning memory and then march bravely into the chitchat. Such a simple, momentarily lapse is so forgivable that it is better to ask for forgiveness than to tell an obvious lie and *not* ask for forgiveness (and of course, you should be forgiving when your name is accidentally forgotten). I am always surprised when an etiquette book suggests elaborate subterfuge when such a situation occurs.

Generally, we address people as they want to be addressed. Many social relationships nowadays start out on a first-name basis. Maybe there's a touch of Great Aunt Vivian in me, but I miss the formality of respect titles (Mr., Miss, and so on) and wish for their return—for lots of reasons. They made the nature of interpersonal relationships clearer, and they allowed your friends and family a nice piece of intimacy that not everyone had a right to: your first name. However, Social Grace, like etiquette itself, must recognize sweeping societal changes and their effects on how people relate to one another. In many cases, I ask new acquaintances to call me by my first name right away—that way, there's no chance of awkwardness if they are unsure. When you introduce a person, it is often helpful to include "Miss," "Mrs.," "Dr."—or whatever the title is, so people will know how to address her. "Ms." is the correct way to address women until they indicate that they would like to be addressed in another way, or by a first name ("Ms." is a recent—and very helpful—addition to our language that has quickly become standard).

We could talk about the weather. Conversation is a skill, yes, but it isn't as difficult as you might think. If you find yourself tongue-tied in social situations or nervous about lengthy pauses in dialogue, consider that chitchat does not have to be all that interesting (indeed, it should be quite mild in situations

Death Is a Fact of Life

Many people find it awkward when, in the middle of a social conversation, someone they're talking to mentions that, for example, his parents are dead. In time, the pain caused by the death of a parent or other loved one does ease, and one is generally able after a while to explain such deaths as simple facts. But death is a big deal—perhaps the biggest deal there is—and even a casual mention of a long-dead loved one should be met with an appropriate response. That response is a brief, simple "I'm sorry" and a sympathetic look. (The correct reply, just for the record, is "Thank you"—not the dreadful, but common, "It's not your fault.") "I'm sorry" is not only a literal apology; it is also a proper way to express sympathy in all sorts of situations.

where you don't have a good idea about the attitudes and beliefs of your conversational partners). You can start by discussing the weather—a neutral topic that can lead in all sorts of pleasing directions (for example, to the weather where the person you're speaking to grew up, which leads to other facts about that place, which leads to the history of that area, which can lead to that region's history—and then the history of the world is open to your discursive delight). To get conversation going, ask basic, inoffensive questions—"Nice day isn't it?" "I like autumn, don't you?" "Are you from this area?" "How do you know our host?"—and follow up with more questions sparked by what was said.

Another tip: If you are very shy, consider preparing some conversational topics to keep in your mental back pocket (good books you have recently read, something interesting but uncontroversial in the news, and so on). Having conversations ready to go may help you feel a bit more confident in social situations.

It is important to not only *have* good manners but also actively communicate that you respect others. This happens in many ways. One is plain speech. Although Great Aunt Vivian and her ilk may pepper their conversation with French terms, for example—just as many modern urbanites overuse jargony "techspeak"—they are more often than not betraying insecurity. Etiquette and style mavens have always insisted that plain, easy-to-understand speech is correct. Well-mannered people *want* to be understood; therefore, they use language that is sure to be accessible to their conversational partners.

By the same token, Social Grace prefers that euphemisms of the more flowery sort be avoided. For example, if you are at a restaurant and you need to find the restrooms, simply ask an employee for the location of the men's room or women's room; in a private home, I think your best bet is asking for directions to the . . . *bathroom*—there, I've said it.

Plain speech should not be graphic, though: you don't tell your hostess exactly what you are going to do there, or that you are going to "use it.") If you simply cannot bear to say the "b-word," I suggest taking a cue from some women—who for years have been excusing themselves to "powder their noses" as cover for everything from natural bodily functions to assassination attempts—and asking your host if there is somewhere you can "wash your hands."

Well-mannered behavior does not preclude plain speech. A properly used euphemism spares us offensive or unpleasant details and prevents the elevation of a something, such as a restroom visit, to something it is not—namely, in this case, cause for comment.

 ## Dead to Me

Dear
Social Grace,

Is it impolite to call a person "dead," or is it better to say "passed away" or something like that?

Dear Undead
Madam or Sir,

When speaking about topics that are unpleasant or difficult to think about, we often employ euphemisms as an emotional buffer. Neither "passed away" nor "dead" is wrong (unless the person being discussed is, in fact, alive), and proponents of plain speech prefer the latter. But although "dead" is one of those four-letter words that one *can* say in polite company, terms such as "passed away" occasionally come in handy when the subject is especially tender. In such a case—if you are having a very hard time choosing words—you might opt for less-direct terminology.

Obey the law and other posted signs. This pertains to things as simple as not jaywalking. We all know the rules, and we have all been irked when else has flouted the law. Hold yourself to the same standards you hold the rest of the world (even when you think no one is looking—haven't you ever seen someone do something wrong, when he thought no one could see him?). We generally know when we are breaking rules—whether the rules of our gym (you know you must wipe down the machines after you use them) or the rules of the office kitchen (you know you ought to wash your own dishes). Do the right thing. It's just safer.

Don't smoke 'em if you've got 'em. Nowadays, you may most often find yourself smoking outside. However, try not to smoke while walking (you have too little control over where your smoke blows behind you, and it may blow right into someone else's face) and keep in mind that, yes, a cigarette end is litter (not only litter but also *litter that is on fire*). Make sure that it is completely extinguished before dropping it into a garbage can or other appropriate receptacle.

Unless you see an ashtray with actual cigarette ends in it, you can probably assume that a person's home is a smoke-free zone. You should not, as a rule, even ask to smoke indoors—just ask if you may step outside for a smoke (your host may invite you to smoke indoors, but more likely, he will frogmarch you to the driveway). Even if you do see an ashtray, you should ask before lighting up.

Be the sort of person you would like to know. Don't gossip. Don't complain. Share your good fortune. Appreciate your friends and family, and treat them with at least as much courtesy as you treat the rest of the world. (Treating family mem-

The Sound of Silence

As we struggle through our difficult days in the urban jungles we call home, we are sure to encounter many people who behave inappropriately toward us. Social Grace gets lots of requests for snappy comebacks: People want to know what to say when, for example, someone says "Excuse me" in an unnecessarily peevish tone as he makes his way off an elevator, what to say when someone at the gym comments disparagingly on the state of one's thighs, or how to respond when a total stranger walks up and asks whether the baby in one's arms is adopted.

❧ The perfect response to these comments—and in many similar situations—has the benefit of being both easy to remember and easy to employ, even when you're terribly flustered: It is silence.

❧ Not responding to a direct question is impolite, yes—here, it's an example of politely applied rudeness. But when a stranger approaches you and begins verbally misbehaving, silence will (a) end the conversation before it has the chance to get any *more* inappropriate, (b) communicate—more clearly than just about anything you could say—the tactlessness of what has just happened, and (c) provide a seamless end to the transaction.

❧ Have fun practicing a few "silent looks" in the mirror at home: there's "perplexed silence," there's "surprised silence," there's "outraged silence"—plenty of variations that you can easily tailor to an infinite number of situations. Forget the snappy comeback (although they are undeniably fun to think about after the fact).

bers—who may be the most exasperating people many of us deal with—with this level of courtesy can be a challenge; you don't have to tell me. But being a good daughter or brother or cousin is a challenge well worth its rewards.) Praise people often. Let others share in the conversation. Be open to learning new things. We did learn all of this stuff in kindergarten, but it bears conscious effort every now and again.

As a modern urbanite makes his way through his beloved city, he is sure to meet people from all over the world. These people may have very different customs, beliefs, and ways of looking at the world. While no etiquette book can prepare you for every person you will meet, the best way to approach unfamiliar situations is to put on your best American manners and to proceed with caution. Don't panic—it is appropriate, when you are in your own country, to follow its etiquette rules until you know that different customs are more appropriate (for example, when a friend from Japan explains that, in her home, guests remove their shoes). When you know in advance that you will be facing unfamiliar customs (for example, if you will be attending a wedding in a Catholic church and you don't know what is appropriate), you can do a bit of research about what will be expected of you in that particular situation.

 ## People—People Who Need Money

Dear
Social Grace,

Has Social Grace yet addressed the etiquette of dealing with homeless people who ask for money? Is it rude to ignore them?

Dear Madam or Sir,

As far as Social Grace is concerned, the operative word in the term *homeless people* is not *homeless* but *people*. Therefore, dealing with homeless people in most cases is not noticeably different from dealing with people who have homes. The way we deal with their direct requests for money (provided, of course, that the requests are put to us in a polite way) should be the same way we deal with other requests from strangers (often other people who want our money, our signatures, or our time): a courteous acknowledgement whether we are refusing the request or not. You may either hand over some change with a smile or reply with an "I'm sorry, no." Of course, attacks and insults are best ignored (no matter whence they come—beggar or celebrity debutante), and it's unwise to engage a person who seems threatening.

Most people have their own ideas about philanthropy—if, when, to whom, and how much to give—and these are entirely personal matters. The questions of poverty and homelessness will not be solved today by Social Grace, but these uncertain and uncomfortable situations are often where good manners are most needed. At its most basic, etiquette serves to ensure respectful treatment for everyone. If we take that principle to heart, we can see that simply ignoring a polite, personal request for spare change is quite obviously wrong.

Everyone deserves your respect and courteous treatment.
Heaven knows, I have woken up on the wrong side of the bed. So I would not dream of suggesting that readers be chirping,

cheerful, happy little birds all the time. But if you cannot be cheerful, at least be solemnly courteous—even if doing so is a bit of an effort. It is worth the trouble (but if you don't try it, you will never know). Whether you are dealing with a stranger you must pass on a crowded subway platform, an acquaintance at the gym, or a coffee-counter cashier, remember that other people enjoy smiles (and have since the dawn of time—many primates share this trait with us). Show yourself to be a person of good manners and a friendly disposition, wherever you go. You may be amazed at whom you impress.

The kind of self-discipline this requires is not easy for some of us. Many folks have learned (illogically) that they, as individuals, are much more important than their society as a whole. They believe (wrongly) that they have a "right" to express every feeling or thought that comes into their heads. They insist (selfishly) that they are entitled to luxurious ease at the expense of others. You may have to re-educate yourself a wee bit.

You may find individual humans exasperating, annoying, and stupid, but you must admit that human civilization has accomplished a few worthwhile things (haiku, rock-and-roll, and cheesecake, just to name a few). Try to see individual humans as representatives of all the good things human civilization has to offer.

That woman at the gym who been on the treadmill for ten minutes past the maximum time allowed? Get her attention and apologetically let her know that she seems to have lost track of the time. That shifty coffee-counter clerk who grudgingly rings up your latte every morning? Force yourself to smile and thank her. And no matter how psychically wounded you feel when you get to work, say "good morning" to that nice security guard, hold the elevator door for other people, refill the office coffee pot, and treat your coworkers with respect. Starting now, be a part of the solution to humanity's rudeness problem.

The Apartment

*Your own safety is at stake when
your neighbor's wall is ablaze.*

—HORACE

iving in a crowded city has advantages, yes—touring companies of hit Broadway shows very rarely make it to Alaskan
fishing villages, and finding a really top-notch tailor in rural
Montana is nearly impossible. But close quarters also require
forbearance and extra effort at cooperation.

The difficult—and often very awkward—intimacy of apartment, loft, or townhouse living can test even the most courteous person. Social Grace knows: he has lived in an apartment
for years. Luckily, there are some ways to nurture peaceful
coexistence—and solve problems *before* anyone wants to set a
neighbor's apartment on fire.

The most important way to have good neighbors is to be a
good neighbor: Pick up that drift of takeout menus in the
lobby, even though other people have been stepping over
them for more than a week. Keep your front step swept, your
fire escape clear of overflowing recycling bins, and so on. The
practical benefit of being an all-around good neighbor is that,

when you accidentally err—say, if a party gets too loud or if your dog ravishes a neighbor's azalea bush—other people are a lot more likely to be forgiving.

And just as important as all that is respecting your neighbors' privacy. Especially in apartment buildings, close urban quarters can make this difficult—but try to let friendships with neighbors happen naturally. Keeping a bit of friendly distance at first is wise.

First things first, meet your neighbors. In an emergency—or if you run out of margarita mix during your next party—you may be very glad that you have established friendly relations. In modern apartment buildings and neighborhoods, a good old-fashioned "Welcome Wagon" is something of a rarity. But although it is generally considered polite for an established resident to make the first move and introduce herself to a new neighbor, the new neighbor can and should introduce himself if this does not happen.

Before you even move in, you can start letting the people around you know how delightfully courteous their new neighbor is. For example, leave a note for the people below your new flat, letting them know when you'll be moving your furniture in and possibly causing a bit of noise as you carry heavy things up the stairs.

Living in close proximity to others requires that we pay extra attention to the noise we make. Certainly, we can agree that a neighbor's reasonable request for quiet should be met with a good-faith attempt to lessen noise. Not all requests will *seem*

Laundry-Room Rules

There are shockingly few "established" etiquette rules for the laundry room, considering how many problems these rooms can pose. It is as if Great Aunt Vivian and her friends had never set foot in one. In the main, we can let common sense be our guide, but a few rules need to be codified. Social Grace is the one to do it:

~ If your building's laundry room has, for example, two washing machines and two dryers, a considerate tenant will use only one of each at a time. (You may even want to work with your landlord or building association to make this an established, and posted, "rule.") Try to leave a fair number of washing machines and dryers free for your neighbors.

~ In a crowded public laundry, be considerate of others. For example, "saving" baskets meant for general use is improper (and selfish). If you see someone doing this when you need a basket, don't be intimidated: Walk up and ask if you might use it for a moment; then return it to that person.

~ If you leave your clothes unattended, be very watchful of the time, so you can return and move them out of the washer and into a dryer promptly (so other people don't have to wait). It's a good idea, too, to leave a laundry basket near the machine you're using, so if you are unexpectedly distracted by an *I Dream of Jeanie* rerun while your laundry is in the basement laundry room, someone can place your wet clothes in the basket, not on the dirty concrete floor that most laundry rooms feature.

~ If you come upon a full washing machine that has completed its cycle, you should wait to see whether the clothes will be claimed before you move them (and you should never move them onto the aforementioned dirty floor). If, after fifteen minutes (this is a reasonable time to wait), the clothes' owner does not materialize, you can, by rights, remove them so that you may begin your own wash. (Put them on top of a machine if no basket is available, or put them in a dryer—but don't start it. Although that may *seem* kind, the load may contain delicate items that have to hang dry.)

reasonable—but the slight creak of a floorboard overhead, say, or the low rumbling of a TV late at night can be maddeningly annoying in the right circumstances. A neighbor's request may seem extreme, but an apology and an honest effort to keep things down may be all she wants or needs: Lay down carpet padding. Move speakers away from shared walls and from floors. Wear soft-soled house shoes when you're at home.

Then check back in with the complaining neighbor to see whether things have improved.

By the same token, certain noises from neighbors' abodes are unavoidable: *One Life to Live* played at normal audio or a ringing phone, for example. If a neighbor seems to be a bit *too* sensitive, apologize, mention your building's strange acoustics, and smilingly explain that you don't know what else you can do. If he persists, you might make your case with the building's manager or co-op board. If a neighbor is harassing you, you need not stand for it.

Small apartments are often inappropriate venues for large, rambunctious cocktail parties. Before you throw your next party, let your neighbors know. You might even sweeten the deal by leaving them a sort of "apology in advance"—in the form of movie passes, for example (this may even get them out of the house on the evening in question). *And let them know when the party will end.* A little bit of excessive noise at 10 p.m. isn't so upsetting if you know that it will end at 10:30 (and if it really does end at that time). Plan ahead to, for example, move to a bar or restaurant to end your party if you're a party-all-night-long sort of person. The hours between 10 p.m. and 6 a.m. are considered "quiet time" (by law in many cities), and extra effort should be made during those hours.

You are responsible for the state of your community. If your neighborhood is a mess—even if you didn't make the mess—think about ways you can clean it up. Many people will quite eagerly confront other folks they perceive to be "acting improperly," and Social Grace gets letters all the time from people who want to know how to "tell off litterers," for example. The answer is, telling people off is very often the wrong thing to do. (It is an etiquette paradox: Telling someone he is rude is, itself, unspeakably rude.) To continue with our example litterer, you *can* politely inquire whether the person is aware that he has dropped something. Be warned that this type of thing can be hard to pull off without sounding peevishly sarcastic and beginning an interaction that leaves a sour taste in the mouths of everyone involved. You should always keep this in mind: You are more than welcome to pick that litter up yourself.

 ## For the Good of the Neighborhood

Dear Social Grace,

In the midst of California's "power emergency," my neighbor has continued her practice of leaving her porch light on all day. I feel as though I should say something to her, but my girlfriend disagrees, saying it's not our business. This neighbor recently reprimanded us for not recycling pizza boxes correctly, so the lines of "neighborly correction" are open—and I honestly think she should be turning her porch light off. So, is it rude for me to say something?

Dear Neighborly Madam or Sir,

Your letter forces us to re-examine the sometimes vague distinction between private and public life. Yes, etiquette wants us to mind our own business. However, the well-being of our community is arguably our own business, because it affects all of us. Etiquette also requires that we turn the other cheek, that we see a difference between what is contrary only to a personally held worldview (and doesn't need your correction) and what is truly bad for everyone (which may).

When our community's health is threatened by an individual's action, we are, perhaps, morally bound to act. Where, then, is the border between private and public?

Does a power shortage make personal power usage public business? Does the depletion of natural resources make personal recycling habits public business?

These are questions for you to ask your conscience. For example, I might mention to a neighbor that her porch light was illuminating the daylight—the greater good here served by an interpersonal "bad"—but I make it a point not to notice my friends' and neighbors' trash. Are you truly acting in the best interest of your community rather than serving a neighborly grudge? If so, you may consider taking steps. The best way to handle your power-wasting neighbor is to assume that the problem is accidental and that she will want to correct it as soon as she hears about it. Getting this to sound convincing might take some practice. Try it out first on your girlfriend to be sure you're coming across as a concerned citizen or friend—not as a vengeful neighbor still peeved about that pizza-box reprimand. The power-waster may thank you and turn off her porch light, she may thank you and ignore your friendly help, or she may simply escalate the communal critique you've got going on in your neighborhood and inform you that you leave takeout menus on your doorstep too long.

Public censure is powerful weapon. Having trouble with an inconsiderate neighbor? Join forces with other concerned community members and pay him a visit. *One* person complaining about Tina Turner at ear-shattering decibels can be dismissed as a kook with poor taste in music. *A group* of people, presenting their concerns in a friendly but stern way, feels more like the law of the land. And if you happen to have, perhaps, unreasonable expectations from your neighbors, speaking with your other neighbors may help you realize it.

Before getting actively involved in a feud with a recalcitrant neighbor, explore gentler options. Speak to a landlord, a rental board, or local law-enforcement if you must deal with a rude neighbor who becomes threatening. The authorities get things done, and they can spare you unpleasant arguments. And this rule can apply not only to the street where you live, but also to any street you find yourself traveling on.

Commuter Conduct

There's nothing under Heaven so blue
That's fairly worth the traveling to.
—ROBERT LOUIS STEVENSON

The bus or subway is a very common place for politely applied rudeness to be required. For it to work, though, you must have started out at a place of friendly good manners. (You are also certain to encounter public-transportation situations in which you simply have to tolerate minor annoyances.)

Public transportation belongs to the public. This would seem obvious, but I have noticed many people who have mistaken my bus line for their own private bathrooms. (Please, gentle commuters, clip your nails *before* you leave the house.) Commuting by bus or rail requires that people reach a group consensus about items such as open windows and the like (failing the intervention of the driver, the local voice of authority). Getting along in public involves cooperation, which requires communication. And keep in mind that a cross-town bus (like other public areas) is hardly the place to seek perfect comfort.

If you see someone who is elderly or burdened with many packages, regardless of the genders of the people involved, give up your seat if you can. When you don't, the people around you see you for the brutish lout that you are, even though you're pretending to be so engrossed in your book (or so "asleep") that you're oblivious to passengers more deserving of seats than you. This is a transparent ruse.

If you are already standing and feel that you must intercede to help a fellow passenger, first ask the seemingly in-need person if he would like a seat. (Don't embarrass him by speaking for him without his permission.) If he wants to sit, you can address the bus as a whole: "Let's see if we can find a seat for you" or "Could someone give this gentleman a seat?" When someone relinquishes a seat, a warm thank you may make that person likelier to give up a seat, without prompting, in the future. (Positive reinforcement works, with dogs and commuters.) If you need a seat and none of the above happens, it is quite appropriate for you to ask for the seat you are due.

Those who ride single in a double seat by taking the outside space may simply be planning a quick exit at the next stop (but, my goodness, does this practice ever irritate a lot of bus riders). Try to give them the benefit of the doubt. Again, a friendly demeanor on your part is key—though this may not be possible when you're dealing with someone who is letting his backpack ride in an empty seat on a crowded bus. Try prefacing "I'd like to sit down" with "Excuse me" or "May I?" and save your icy stare for the person who answers, "Oh, my bag is in this seat." (I saw it happen.)

The thing is, there's only the merest chance that true seat-hogs don't know that they're being selfish. *They don't care*, and no amount of your disapproval will make them care. We live on this planet with a few inconsiderate people, and they are easier to deal with if you keep your own good manners operational.

There are a few ways to handle rude passengers on public transportation. Most people reading this book, I'd imagine, need only gentle reminders about bus-riding etiquette, if that. Their more immediate concerns involve handling impolite others.

The first thing you must do is look within yourself to see whether you are facing a tolerable annoyance. For example, if a person next to you is chewing gum very loudly (a ghastly habit, to be sure), it is not your place to correct her. But what if that person also has her stereo turned up to maximum volume? Or is eating sunflower seeds and spitting the husks onto the floor?

First, realize that this person *wants* to get your negative attention—refusing to give it to her is one way to thwart her. And that loud music may even help you—by preventing you from falling asleep in your seat and missing your stop.

But if, for example, that music consists largely of words that polite people just do not use, then you may have a problem that something needs to be done about. Your first step should be to give her a chance to behave herself. Treat her with the courtesy you expect from her: Ask whether she could turn her music off.

If that doesn't work, alert the bus driver. Many people hesitate to go to the authorities, but if the situation has reached this point, you are likely dealing with someone who is dangerously antisocial, and you are wise to avoid embroiling yourself in a shouting match.

The bus driver may not want to help—in which case, you may release frustration in a time-honored and perfectly polite way: by complaining to the bus company's management, your city councilperson, or anyone else who may have an interest in shabby service on a public conveyance.

 ## Do Not Disturb

Dear
Social Grace,

I'm an avid reader, but I have very little time to enjoy reading. In fact, usually my only opportunities come during my lunch break and my commute. When I'm reading, I put in brightly colored earplugs and become so deeply engrossed in my book that I may as well hang a "Do Not Disturb" sign around my neck. However, several times a week, some coworker or acquaintance seems to take my reading as a sign that I'm just lonely and would really prefer to talk to someone. Then I feel obligated to be attentive and join him or her in small talk. Now, I may be coming across as stuck-up, but believe me, when genuine conversation comes along, I'm happy to put down my book and have a nice talk. These folks, though, while good-hearted, don't really have anything to say; they just jabber on about the weather, or about how someone else they know jabbers to them about the weather and how much they dislike it.

When I'm approached on public transit, it becomes especially awkward, since they ask where I'll be getting off and expect my full attention until that point, thus neatly cornering me. Is there something I'm doing that invites this, or do I just know a lot of lonely people? And when I see someone I know, regardless of how close I am to them or how distracted they look, is it my social duty to get their attention and engage them in conversation? I feel as though I may have missed an etiquette lesson here somewhere.

Dear Literary Madam or Sir,

Some people **prefer conversation to reading, and there** are limits to the privacy one can expect in a public place (even with earplugs). Neither your attitude nor the attitude of your chatty acquaintances is "wrong." You are not required to engage every acquaintance you see in conversation; however, ignoring a person, especially if he notices you ignoring him, comes dangerously close to the ultimate public censure, "cutting" someone "dead" (that is, looking right through him as if he were unknown to you). This is powerful stuff, to be reserved for the worst of the worst.

What you seek is companionable silence. Though it will cost you a minute or two of book time, it's quite easy to achieve. Simply make it clear that that's what you want. Start with a greeting, follow that with some variation of "you're looking well," and then move to the good-byes. "Give my regards to Rebecca; I hope I'll see you soon" works on the bus, for example. You might even toss in an "I can't tear myself away from this book." Then, after smiles all around, insert your earplugs and return to your book, social obligation fulfilled.

When riding on escalators and people movers, we stand on the right and pass on the left. And we try to keep the right when we are walking on public sidewalks and in hallways, just as if we were driving.

Drivers are people, too. While many modern urbanites must—for reasons of expense, lack of parking, and so on—forgo the pleasures of operating a private automobile, some of us do enjoy that privilege.

Drivers are already governed by numerous laws. But etiquette has its place on our freeways and streets. "Road rage" has become a particular problem in some areas because, like the Internet, a car can give a person a sense of anonymity.

An important part of driving defensively—unfortunately, a part left out of most high-school driving-education classes—is to allow others to make mistakes without getting too upset about it. While some in-car muttering is understandable and often quite satisfying, working yourself into a tizzy over others' driving skills (or lack thereof) doesn't help anyone. Etiquette serves to help you maintain your dignity. The minute you stoop to rude hand gestures or shouted epithets, your dignity is severely compromised.

Not all drivers who frustrate us do so through simple error, though. Some drivers are just plain mean and nasty. It has happened to all of us: a driver, usually going dangerously fast, cuts your car off, proceeds to endanger your life in some way, and then starts shouting and making hand gestures at you.

This is another place where *silence* may be your best response. The *first* response that comes to most people's minds (I know I can speak for myself here) is to give back more of the same. But before you do that, stop and consider this: These driving "bullies" *want* to get a rise out of you. Ignore a bully, and you ruin his day (this is true of many situations, not just when you're in a car). Alert the authorities—by calling the police non-emergency number and giving them the license-plate number of this reckless driver—and the problem may actually be addressed.

 ## Breaking the Road Rules

Dear
Social Grace,

While driving in to work last week, I accidentally cut off a coworker of mine. She is usually quite friendly at the office, but in this instance, she honked at me several times, sped up to pass me, and made what I guess you would call a "rude hand gesture." I was shocked! And I was a little bit hurt, too. Her behavior toward me at the office, though, was the same, and I assume that she did not recognize me or my car. I feel like I want to say something to her about this, because the more I think about it, the more I'm upset by her rude behavior. Is this something I should just forget about, or is there something I could say?

Dear Shocked Madam or Sir, Your coworker was not only terribly careless but also aggressively mean and nasty. Shame on her. Perhaps you can dissuade your coworker of the notion (widely held though it may be) that being in a car gives a person the permission to be rude. Don't start off with an attack, though. You should give her a chance to apologize, by doing the same yourself (you may need to practice making it sound believable): "I'm sorry I cut you off yesterday morning at the corner of Third and Market; I didn't see your car." If she has any sense, she'll be mortified by her inappropriate response to such a common, accidental occurrence, and she might be more careful with her motoring manners in the future.

Even from the driver's seat of your car, you should own up to and apologize for your mistakes. An apologetic expression or a pantomimed "I'm sorry" may help calm another driver's incipient road rage.

Life is a journey. It is sometimes said that the journey is more important than the destination. That may not always be the case, but we owe it to ourselves—and to others—to work a bit to make the journey bearable, so we can be at our best when we arrive at wherever it is we are going.

The Play's the Thing

I have often regretted my speech, never my silence.
—PUBLILIUS SYRUS

Venues devoted to public entertainment are, in some ways, like vehicles of public transportation. For example, the privilege of enjoying them requires that we put an entire group's comfort before any individual's comfort, even if that means that some individuals will be unable to do *exactly* as they please. Audiences are what make public entertainment possible, so treat them with respect. (Luckily, personal home-entertainment technology has made incredible advances in recent years. If you can't treat audiences with respect, you can probably enjoy yourself just as well at home.)

Never has so much entertainment been available to humankind: A musical experience that would have been a once-in-a-lifetime event for our great-grandparents is readily available to us for $8.99 at the local megastore (or for free elsewhere). The type of acted performances our great-grandparents could only read about are ours to enjoy at the cinema for less than many people pay for lunch. Because these things come to us so inexpensively, they can be easy to treat as background noise. Deadened to nuance by the constant availability of tunes and the omnipresence of video screens, many people may need some help recognizing performances that require attention and respectful behavior. (We draw distinctions, of course, between a Metallica concert, where one should expect a little ambient noise from the crowd, and a chamber music recital, where audience participation is less integral to the overall experience.)

If someone is being too loud at a performance or at the movies, you may take action. First, try a look. (See if you can channel Great Aunt Vivian for just a moment.) Then try a soft "shhh" or even a whispered request ("Please be quiet; we can't hear the film")—when we ask a fellow audience member to be quiet, we must do so politely. (Some of us may need to practice "politely" at home before trying it out in public. Remember that it never involves calling someone else rude or making comments on his character.) If that fails, you can try a sterner request ("I must ask you again to be quiet"). If the noise continues, seek out an usher.

At a recent performance of a touring musical production, I had the unpleasant experience of sitting next to a woman who insisted on singing along with the performers. After concerned looks failed, I politely asked her to desist. She ignored me, and her companion turned to me and said, explanatorily, "Oh, she loves to sing."

"Well," I thought to myself, "how nice for her." I then sought out an usher and asked to be reseated. As that wasn't possible, the usher used her considerable authority to shut the woman up, explaining that "people had been complaining." Dealing with such people in an audience is part of an usher's job, and in cases like this one, you should seek one out. If the usher refuses, become a very demanding customer, indeed: Ask for a manager, and ask for the price of your ticket to be refunded.

Most people go to movies, concerts, and the like to see and hear performers—not other audience members. Talking and making other noise during such a performance is impolite. Period. When someone "shushes" you at the movies, the correct response is not "Shush yourself." It is "I'm so sorry"—or better yet, an apologetic look and an immediate cessation of noise.

There is rarely a need to applaud a film. Applause is how we show appreciation for performers. In a film, the performers cannot hear you applaud—and more importantly, they cannot hold their next lines until applause has ended, as stage performers do. This is why it is not customary to applaud at the cinema. Doing so drowns out the film's audio and thus disturbs those around you. If, however, you are attending a special performance and the filmmakers or performers are in attendance, you might express your enjoyment by applauding at the film's end.

By the same token, expressing displeasure to a film—by booing or hissing, for example, is plainly a ridiculous thing to do if one stops to think about it for just a moment.

If you are expecting an urgent telephone call (if a life is at stake, say), you should, perhaps, think about forgoing the pleasures of a movie, opera, play, or concert. That way, the urgent call is certain to be received, and other people will not be disturbed by a digital rendition of "Ode to Joy" while trying to enjoy an orchestral arrangement of the same. I know some of you may be saying to yourself right now, "My calls are important—I have to take my phone with me." However, as students of etiquette, we have to remember that consideration for other people is just as important. And I know we've all heard one side of at least one ill-timed cell-phone conversation that was not remotely close to a life-or-death situation.

Is it immoral or impolite to save a seat in a crowded movie theater? No, it isn't—if we are talking about one seat, for a few minutes, while your date goes off to fetch some Junior Mints. There is, however, something wrong with showing up at the cinema on the opening weekend of a summer blockbuster with a dozen homemade "Reserved" signs that you use to save prime seats for friends who didn't put in queue time with everyone else. Obviously, that is just not fair.

Not all theater-going experiences are enjoyable. It is customary to express violent displeasure with a performance in a verbal way. Boos and hisses, of course, should be reserved for the worst of the worst—for truly offensive material. And you are welcome to express this kind of displeasure only very briefly. Thereafter, you should be prepared leave the theater so anyone who is enjoying the event may continue to do so. Indeed, a silent retreat is a much more elegant way to communicate your displeasure.

The Play Was *Not* the Thing

Dear
Social Grace,

I had the misfortune of seeing a horrible play last week. My boyfriend, though, would not allow us to leave, saying that it would be rude to the actors. Is it really rude to leave a play that you are not enjoying? This is a sore subject for us that has come up more than once.

Dear
Theatergoing
Madam or Sir,

If you leave without disturbing other people in the audience, and if you don't actually know the performers and artists involved, it is not impolite to exit a play during the performance. It's customary to wait quietly until intermission—unless the performance is mightily offensive or so bad as to cause you physical pain. (People who attend the theater regularly know that such a reaction is not unheard-of.)

The audience has an important, and too often disregarded, role in any performance. Take pride in your role, and play your part well. If you can't do at least that, you simply are not ready to share the spotlight.

Other People's Lives

Who could deny that privacy is a jewel?
—PHYLLIS MCGINLEY

It's a concept that many modern people have a hard time getting their mind around: Much of what other people do *is none of our business whatsoever.* For many reasons—the booming popularity of "reality" TV shows, the increasing tendency of "news" outlets to pander to people's more prurient curiosity about celebrities, the rise in the number of people who have benefited from talk therapy, and so on—lots of folks have lost any sense of when to keep their questions and opinions to themselves.

And as important as learning what is strictly others' business is learning what business is strictly our own. You "let it all hang out" at the risk of disturbing, disgusting, or—perhaps worst of all—boring the people you talk to. If you are unable to gain and maintain a certain level of discretion and circumspection, you will be thought of as that dreaded creature, despised by Great Aunt Vivian and Social Grace alike (detested by almost everyone, in fact): a *buttinsky.*

Don't Mention It

Smart socializers will avoid the following topics with new or casual acquaintances:

- money
- politics
- mean-spirited gossip about people not present (in fact, an excellent way to become known as a person of strong moral fiber is to stand up for absent acquaintances who are being dished)
- venomous complaints about almost anything
- sexual behavior
- medical situations
- bathroom situations
- jokes that target a certain ethnicity (or religion, gender, and so on)
- our dreams (frankly, no one is interested).

And socializers who are even smarter will avoid many of these topics within the hearing of other people.

A buttinsky can't tell the difference between a neighbor who is actively harming him (by dumping toxic waste down a public sewer, say) and one who is merely annoying him (by painting his home a particularly bilious shade of mint green), and feels that he has the right to intervene in both cases. A buttinsky behaves as if she were Barbara Walters among a population of troubled movie actors, whom she can interview at will about the most private parts of their lives.

A buttinsky blithely leaves enemies in her wake. Here are a few things to keep in mind, so you can avoid becoming one.

Money is a taboo topic in most social situations. You introduce the topic of personal finances up at your extreme peril. Money should be discussed only with your intimates. Asking someone how much money he makes or how much he paid for an item (nosy!) and divulging that information yourself (showoff!) are to be avoided. Being polite in the United States demands financial egalitarianism. In *theory*, our incomes do not matter—rich and poor are treated the same. In reality, of course, this is often not the case. But we like to think that everyone is making an effort. Asking about a person's finances might seem to indicate that we need to know her income before we can properly relate to her—whether or not this is truly the case.

For the same reason, many people bristle at the very common "What do you do for a living?" line of questioning when it occurs too soon in a casual conversation. There are those who feel that a job (or lack thereof) is not a good indication of character, and rightly so. I've heard, and liked, the alternative phrase "How do you spend your days?" used as a getting-to-know-you chitchat alternative.

Be very careful about criticizing anything in a mean-spirited way. This does not mean that you have to be a Pollyanna all the time. But when a person "puts his foot in his mouth," it is often because he has said something nasty to the wrong person. Imagine it: You're at a party, and a criminally overplayed song by the teen sensation of the moment, Limonada Whistler, begins to play. "Oh!" you exclaim, "This song drives me batty! That Limonada is a silicone-injected, digitally remixed, talentless tramp with all the charisma of a sea sponge."

How could you possibly have known that Limonada's beloved older brother was standing, within earshot, by the punch bowl?

This is an extreme example (and I heard something very similar happen at a party), but it illuminates a very important idea: Think before you excoriate people or things. Ask yourself whether you really know the people you are talking to well enough to say, for example, that "yoga is for people who aren't good at *real* sports" or "country music is just stupid" or "television is for brain-dead idiots." You might just decide to keep your trap shut.

And the fact is, *understatement*—"yoga doesn't look difficult to me" or "I've never understood country music's appeal"— not only is a mark of a cultured person with a keen intellect, but also opens up the possibility of learning something new. People who share your views will know what you mean. People who do not share your views will feel free to enter into a discussion with you, which may actually change your opinion— blatantly negative statements are conversational nonstarters. Learning how to express a negative opinion without insulting anyone is an invaluable skill, because there are so many instances where expressing negative opinions is necessary. Try discussing your opinions as *opinions,* not as irrefutable fact. And keep in mind that there's nothing wrong with discussing the weather if all else fails, or if someone you're speaking to insists on making sour, all-negative statements of his own. I've resorted to this handy topic many times.

Another great way to "put your foot in it" is to make comments on someone's appearance. Even if you are being complimentary, the topic of how someone looks is off limits (by law) in most workplaces (modeling agencies are an obvious exception), and is to be treated warily in most other situations. You may think that "You look great—you must've lost 40 pounds!" is a compliment. To someone who is losing weight owing to an illness, it is most definitely not. (Of course, friends and other people who know each other well have a lot more leeway in this area—and such compliments can certainly be lovely to give.)

And never comment on a woman's pregnancy unless you know for a fact that she is pregnant. You can make a lifelong enemy this way.

Battle of the Buttinsky

Dear
Social Grace,

In the past two months, I've been approached by perfect strangers and subjected to that most obtrusive of questions: "Are you pregnant?" Although I've been cursed with a slight potbelly (courtesy of my father's genes), I am by no means overweight or even overtly rotund. I cannot understand why strangers feel the need to inquire about my reproductive health. I would never dream of asking any woman I did not know intimately whether or not she were expecting—I consider it invasive, if not downright rude.

Please, could you provide me with some gracious yet firm responses to these clumsy questions? In every case, it has been a lose-lose situation, as my *original embarrassment at being asked is further compounded by the questioner's chagrin. How can I reply to questions about my due date, short of "It's none of your business" or "Oh, in about five years—why do you ask?"*

Dear Unexpectant Madam,

Making uninvited comments about another person's physical appearance is a *dangerous* enterprise. People who do so have earned their chagrin, and it'll probably do them some good (after asking about a nonexistent pregnancy, most folks won't make the same mistake again). Don't be too hard on yourself for doling out some much-needed manners correction.

When you're on the receiving end of such a question, tailor your response to the degree of the error. An inappropriate but well-intentioned remark warrants gentler correction. The queries you've gotten might fall into that category, and I don't think you could do better than "Oh, I'm not pregnant." You might even follow that with a long, cool, silent stare, to give the questioner time to realize how inappropriate his question was. Let the horror of it all sink in. I like your second suggestion—a bit of stinging humor might sharpen the lesson. But I warn you that sarcasm is difficult to pull off without sounding unattractively peevish; plus, it is just lost on many people. If you do use that tactic, pause for a minute of silence, and then change the subject or wish your interrogator a chilly good day.

Unsolicited "constructive" personal criticism is the purview of very, very close relatives (such as parents and significant others) and, in the workplace, managers (who may offer their critique only on job-related matters). You may have lots of advice about how others should train their pets, do their hair, decorate their homes, and so on. But unless you are asked, you should keep this advice to yourself. (And really, why give your great advice away for free?) And even when you are asked for it, good criticism is never unkind.

 ## Little White Lies

Dear
Social Grace,

If a very close friend asks you if she looks too fat, and she has in fact been gaining weight by the week, should you say yes or should you lie? The first seems as though it would be more honest and actually helpful, but the second seems nicer. I think it would benefit a certain friend of mine to hear the truth.

Dear Honest
Madam or Sir,

As wonderful as honesty is, and as much as we cherish friends who can be trusted to give it to us, it isn't always the best policy. The answer to your friend's question depends on its timing.

Say your friend—we'll call her Taffy—is preparing for a date with a gentleman she's had a crush on for months. She's bought a new dress, she's spent an hour on her hair, and she's been primping in front of the mirror for 45 minutes. Nervous about the evening, she turns to you and says, "Tell me the truth; do I look too fat?"

What Taffy wants in this situation is probably not bru-tal honesty. What she wants is reassurance, and the best answer would be "Taffy, you look absolutely gorgeous." Taffy almost certainly knows what she looks like, and a long talk about the benefits of this or that diet is not going to help her as she waits for her beau to arrive.

Another example: You and Taffy are having a hair-down, shoes-off heart-to-heart about the meaning of it all, in the middle of which Taffy asks, "Tell me the truth; do I look too fat?"

This is where you can be honest—keeping in mind that honesty doesn't have to be cruel, and the honesty that's "good for us" *never* is. Try this: "You know how lovely I think you are, but if you're worried about gaining weight, maybe I can help. We could go for walks while we have our Sunday heart-to-hearts."

That's gentle and truthful, and there's nothing there to offend Taffy. (A secondary lesson in all of this is that we shouldn't ask our friends to be honest with us if we don't *really* want them to be.) A true friend will then revis-it the subject of Taffy's weight only if Taffy does.

When you have a secret, keep it. When you dish dirt, you invariably get yourself at least a little bit dirty.

 ## Don't I Know You from Somewhere?

Dear
Social Grace, *I am a gay male, and I recently ran into a straight female coworker/friend, who was with a guy who she introduced as her "boyfriend." The problem is, I, uh,*

know this guy very intimately, from a couple of years ago, and I've seen him around in gay bars since our very brief, uh, acquaintance. He did not acknowledge that he recognized me when my friend introduced us, though. My question is, should I tell my coworker that her boyfriend may not be who he says he is?

Dear
Intimate Sir,

The short answer to your question is no. Such a disclosure would be not only inappropriate but also potentially humiliating for your friend. In addition, it assumes many things that are plainly none of your business. For example, who's to say that she doesn't already know?

Nice people don't discuss their intimate knowledge of a new boyfriend's past. The new boyfriend has to explain those things himself. (Besides, just about everyone who's had a boyfriend already knows that what the new ones say about their pasts can't always be taken as the plain truth—your friend doesn't need your warnings.) You are not obligated, however, to participate in social charades perpetuated by rogue "boyfriends": Now that you've been reintroduced, feel free to mention your mutual friend the next time you see this fellow "out and about."

When you are introduced to someone you think you already know, it's not wrong to ask if perhaps you do (unless you know him through your involvement with the CIA, AA, the Witness Protection Program, or another organization that guards the identities of its members). If he demurs, you should at least pretend to have been mistaken. I would see nothing wrong, though, with pressing

61

the point if you thought your friend was in some sort of danger (if, for example, you knew about the man's history of wiping out girlfriends' checking accounts rather than about his sexual history).

Well, actually, there is one way you can get involved in the lives of others. Volunteer. Find a community or nonprofit organization whose goals inspire you, and devote some time to it. You owe it to your city and yourself: you'll not only feel good about those few hours a month you spend in the service of others, but also gain invaluable experience, friends, and even business contacts.

The Art of the Subject Change

*The test of good manners
is to be patient with bad ones.*
—SOLOMON IBN GABIROL

I t has happened to us all: In the middle of a perfectly love-ly dinner, a friend recounts his last trip to the emergency room—in unfortunately gory detail. Or at a party, a new acquaintance asks how much you paid for your shoes. Or at the office water cooler, a coworker inquires as to why you are getting a divorce. And there you are—stuck in an awkward moment.

Because we cannot always rely on other people's tact, a modern urbanite will not be able to maneuver through city life unless he can swiftly, tactfully *change the subject* when the situation calls for it. In many situations where a subject change is right, indignant protests are unnecessary (people often pry because they just don't know any better).

To prying questions, the best first response is a gentle subject change. Simply answer the question you wish you'd been asked. The next time a coworker asks you how much you make or starts describing his kingly signing bonus, for example, pretend that you've heard a more appropriate question and then respond to it. For example: "How much of a raise did you get this year?" could be met with "Yes, the company is growing fast. I hear they're planning an office in Singapore. Have you ever been there?" When deflecting well-intentioned but inappropriate personal questions, simply aim for something you do want to discuss.

If the questioner persists, you may have to be a bit more frank. You can say this with a smile: "Oh, I'm sure that wouldn't interest you at all—it's just my *own personal* business.

 ## Qué Será Será

Dear Social Grace,

I am a woman; however, I wasn't always. I'm quite happy, but I have a problem with talking about my past: I know lying is wrong, but I also don't like to tell people that I was once biologically a male (or even to talk about it, if they already know)—for many obvious and many very private reasons. But it comes up a lot. For example, what do I do when I'm asked about my childhood? Is it rude of me to lie and talk about "when I was just a little girl"?

Dear Madam,

If you want to withhold certain aspects of your life—such as the fact that you underwent a major medical procedure (exactly the type of revelation that many people quite correctly reserve for their closest intimates)—you have every right to do so, and etiquette is solidly on your side. When asked about aspects of your life you'd rather not explain, you might gracefully change the subject. If pressed, you should simply say that you prefer not to discuss your childhood. It is your right to say so.

You should also be able to jump in and put a derailed conversation back on track. Imagine: you're at a restaurant with a group of friends, and someone begins an ill-timed story of an inappropriate nature—and continues, oblivious to everyone's expressions of horror (and even to your gentle kicks under the table). Here are three easily customizable steps to a routine mealtime subject change:

Step One: Intercept. When the speaker pauses in his story—at a point that, for decency's sake, should be the tale's end—jump in and finish it for him. "Oh," you say, with a note of finality and a look of dismay/shock/horror, "how unfortunate/bizarre/terrible."

Step Two: Run with the ball. There are a few topics readily at hand if you're dining in a restaurant, and you should be able to spin any of them for a few minutes—long enough for a speaker to reconsider his topic or at least be distracted from it. "Well," you could say with a smile, "how's your gnocchi/sushi/taco? Mine is just delicious. Have you eaten at that new Italian/Japanese/Mexican place over on 24th/Jane/Lake Street? The one by the dry-cleaning place? Well, it's fabulous. I like that neighborhood, don't you?"

You could also, if you're prepared with a story, launch it by saying: "That reminds me of another interesting story I just heard."

Step Three: Pass. Someone else likely feels the same level of discomfort that you do (if no one does, your conversation-rescue efforts were sort of in vain). He or she is your ally, and together you can get any number of conversations going from your simple opener (although you can hope that your indecorous speaker has come to his senses by now). You might choose to chat about restaurants, international food trends, the merits of neighborhoods, or even dry cleaners (but be careful—"difficult stains" is a topic that could lead you into another dangerous area).

 ## Parent Trap

*Dear
Social Grace,*

My father has a horrible habit of bringing up politics at family gatherings and then attacking people for not sharing his conservative point of view. He'll do this in the middle of otherwise amicable conversations, and it completely kills the mood: Mom goes silent, guests look uncomfortable—I can't tell you how many birthdays/holidays/dinners this has ruined. He used to be tolerable, but he's grown increasingly strident over the past year, and I'm not sure how to put a stop to it. Respectfully disagreeing has been tried, and even staying completely neutral to just preserve what decorum remains, but he keeps trying to push his views down other people's throats (and he's not above personal insults, either). When I've come straight out and asked him to please keep his opinions to himself, he says he's "educating" everyone. I would have loved to have a close father-daughter relationship, but this just makes me dread talking to him at all. Help!

Dear Family-Valuing Madam, If his daughter's pleas, his wife's silence, and his guests' discomfort have had no effect, I'm afraid there's not a whole lot Social Grace can do. Proper etiquette—polite subject changes, agreeing to disagree, private familial discussion—isn't working with your father. That, along with his increasing stridency and personal attacks, leads me to suspect that the problem is something greater than bad manners. Your father sounds like a man who needs professional help. Unfortunately, he also sounds like a fellow who wouldn't agree placidly with such a notion.

Not every familial relationship is pleasant. You and your kin could strive to enjoy yourselves around his diatribes. Sometimes cheerfully agreeing with such a person helps: "I guess you're right, Dad; we really should overthrow Iceland's government and end their monopoly on cod. Do you want more potatoes?" Some families go on for decades like that—once you settle into it, it's not so bad, I hear. And bizarre parental antics can make for interesting stories (or even best-selling memoirs).

Etiquette does have stronger ways to deal with people who are incorrigibly rude, mean, and insulting, and you may someday choose to employ them. Such a conversation might go like this: "I love you, Dad, but you've gone too far. I will not be insulted in front of my friends and family." And then don't be. Let him apologize, if he will, or find friendlier dinner companions. This is a severe solution, one not to be entered into lightly. But although etiquette puts a premium on cherishing family and respecting elders, it also insists that no one has the right to make us too miserable.

Shhh! You may want to add an emphatic "Oh no, you did not go there!" to your subject change. Here, too, silence can speak volumes. Let your inappropriate conversation partner enjoy moment of silence, accompanied by a level stare, before you begin speaking again.

If an off-limits personal topic has proved in the past to be irresistible to acquaintances, you could also try to save people from themselves. Say you've recently broken off an engagement and prefer not to discuss the details with all the nosy parkers who have asked about it. When the subject first comes up, you could simply say, "And you just wouldn't believe the horribly inappropriate questions some nosy people have been asking me."

Such methods can prevent improper queries—and they have the added benefit of complimenting the person you're speaking to.

Scoundrels!

When you have to kill a man, it costs nothing to be polite.
—SIR WINSTON CHURCHILL

People sometimes accuse etiquette of being "hypocritical" because, yes, it does ask that you be polite and nice, even if you are not in an especially nice mood, to the people you encounter as you make your way through life: It wants you to do a little bit of the hard work of keeping the peace on your block, in your community, or on the freeway. Proper etiquette asks that you do your best to ignore many kinds of unpleasant behavior. Believe me, I know that it is not always easy.

But I assure you that etiquette in no way wants you to let yourself be treated *too* shabbily. In fact, Social Grace insists that you refuse to put up with snobs, bullies, gossips, bigots, and other immoral meanies. Yes, you must be nice to everyone—until they demonstrate beyond any shadow of a doubt that they do not intend to do the same. Etiquette gives you some handy tools for dealing with scoundrels.

And when you must deal with someone who has mightily mistreated you, good manners can really pay off. The person with perfect manners has some moral weight to throw around, for one thing.

There are a few people out there who do not deserve polite treatment at all (a very few—you can't apply these punishments to everyone who simply irks you for some reason; if you do, they lose their potency). When a person refuses to play by the rules of a community, that community can and should bring him into line—and with etiquette, or even some politely applied rudeness, you won't even need to storm his house waving pitchforks and torches.

First, learn to differentiate between true scoundrels and people who just have opinions that are different from yours. Central to living in a democratic society (our great good fortune) is being able to politely disagree. When the conversation turns to politics and similar areas, disagreements can get altogether too nasty very quickly. If you can't enter into political discussions without calling into question the humanity and/or parentage of people who disagree with you, you really shouldn't go in for political discussions at all. Let's all take a deep breath before we, for example, call a conservative Republican a "fascist" or label a Green-party liberal a "moron." (Although Social Grace has been known to share a few choice words with local politicians, he does so only when no one can really hear him—when those politicians appear on the nightly news, for example. This has proved to be a very effective way of handling feelings of frustrated anger.) For many people, remembering that others' opinions are *different,* not *wrong* (and therefore not in need of being corrected) will take an effort. When you encounter someone of a different political bent, say, do your best to find out *why* he feels the way he does. Try to ask lots of genuine questions (the answers, at least, will help your prepare for your next debate).

If you can, ask questions not only about other people's views but also about other areas of their lives. You may find you have other things in common, and that will provide a graceful subject change. Social Grace has very friendly relationships with lots of people whom he has had to "agree to disagree" with, about topics as important to him as silver polish and capital punishment.

 ## God Only Knows

Dear
Social Grace,

I am an entrenched atheist, and living in a big city, I am generally left in peace and not bothered too much by God-mongers. However, in recent weeks, I find myself encountering talk of God at every corner, even from normally sane people who have never before shown any interest in religion or its trappings. At a small dinner party I attended at a friend's house, a friend asked her guests to clasp hands, bow their heads, and join her in a silent prayer before dinner. I clasped and bowed, but not without some disgust at myself for playing along in what I consider a fool's game. How else could I have responded?

Dear Godless Madam or Sir, If prayer doesn't appeal, there are lots of things one might do while bowing one's head and clasping hands with a neighbor: prepare a grocery list, multiply 1,209 by 367, woolgather. You might even *hope* for the kinds of things that others may be praying for. Any of these activities would be respectful of a friend's desire for quiet prayer but wouldn't compromise your personal beliefs.

When it comes to differences of religion, etiquette asks us to have a bit of humility—at the very least to pretend to believe that people with different views are just that, rather than "insane" or "participating in a fool's game." It asks us to compromise, to show respect for others' religions, and to allow them to practice as they see fit. Your friend's request for silent prayer sounds like an effort at compromise or inclusion, the kind of effort I like to hear about. In response, you did the correct thing. Short of declining all invitations to socialize with people who do not share your beliefs, I don't know what else you could do.

One type of scoundrel is someone whose talk or jokes denigrate others based on their race, nationality, religion, gender, sexuality, political affiliation, and so on. When someone you must speak with begins such nastiness, you should do what you can to correct him. Here are a few handy phrases you can keep in your pocket to pull out in case of such emergencies:

- "I don't think you meant that to sound the way it did. Surely, you couldn't mean...."
- "I'm not sure why you think that joke is funny."

■ "I'm sorry; I will not listen to that kind of talk." (And then don't listen to it. Leave the room if you have to.)

No matter how convivial the conversation has been, when racist talk, for example, is introduced, social pleasantries are at an end. You can (indeed, as a force for civilization, you *must*) state plainly and firmly that you will not listen to such language. Done correctly, in an even tone and without resorting to argument or name-calling, this *is* the polite thing to do. Thereafter, you'll very often be required to listen to squirming apologies of the "I didn't mean anything by it" sort—which I rather enjoy, and which I tend to accept as frostily as possible.

 ## The N-Word

Dear Social Grace,

You've tackled the issue of racism, specifically in regard to someone who uses the "n-word," and you suggested promptly cutting off any conversation with the offending individual, which makes sense, but what if that individual happens to be your supervisor or a coworker?

Dear Concerned Madam or Sir,

When someone you know—be he coworker, friend, or Uncle Mortimer—starts speaking in a highly offensive manner, you can address the problem just as firmly, if with a bit more politesse. You still want to indicate that such talk is intolerable, but you might pretend to believe that the person in question misspoke. Allow yourself a shocked silence before exclaiming, "That sounded *absolutely* unforgivable. I'm *sure* it didn't come out the way you intended." If that doesn't work, you must explain, as curtly as you like, that you cannot participate in such conversations.

A coworker with any sense whatsoever is going to put as much distance between himself and any racial slurs he might have uttered—which are illegal in the workplace, I'll just note—as he can. If he doesn't, and if the environment at your workplace is noticeably bigoted, I recommend that you speak to your personnel department, a manager, or a labor lawyer right away.

People who are childishly rude or insulting are "minor scoundrels." I liken them to mosquitoes. People who are rude or insulting, but not actively threatening, are best ignored. You can also try treating them with uncomprehending politeness. For one thing, treating someone as if he were polite can often make him so. And for another, it is very frustrating to a minor scoundrel when her "witty" sarcastic comments are not understood.

Customer Disservice

Dear Social Grace,

I'm hoping you might help me with a dilemma I encountered during a recent shopping experience. I had a long airport layover and decided to pass the time in one of those overpriced concourse shops. Upon trying on what appeared to be a unisex raincoat (I am a man), I heard a squeal from inside the shop and looked up, only to hear the reverberating exclamation, "Oh my God! That's a WOMAN'S jacket!" from the apparent love child of a poodle and a Kewpie doll.

Checking the impulse to counter with, "And that's a bad home perm!" I simply shrugged my shoulders and replaced it on the rack. After browsing a short while more, I considered taking the salesgirl aside and instructing her in proper customer-service etiquette, but she had gone on break. Social, what is the proper response to poor treatment in this or any other situation in which one is the party paying?

Dear Paying Sir,

As Grandmother Grace might say, trying to teach manners to a clueless sales clerk is like trying to teach the fox trot to a pig—it wastes your time, and it only annoys the pig. And instructing this woman in proper etiquette is neither your responsibility nor your place. Aside from the fact that such instruction almost always falls on deaf ears, there's almost no way to tell a stranger that she has been rude without being rude yourself.

What is your recourse in this situation? Find a supervisor or a manager, and explain politely why you will not be buying anything at Runway Fashions. Write a letter. Make a phone call. You can probably even send an e-mail. This way, you might actually locate someone who cares (or who pretends to care) about the behavior of sales clerks. You'll feel better, and the problem might somehow be addressed.

Your handling of this salesperson was just right. That instinct that told you to refrain from making personal comments was a good one. A cool nod and a very slight grin might be just the thing in a situation such as this, but I've found that many people magically *become* polite when you treat them as if they already were. If I had been in your place, I might have smiled handsomely and said, "And it's a very nice fabric. Do you have it in blue?"

Behavior that puts others in danger is unacceptable. Dealing with idiots can be difficult. As much as I hate to admit it, you and I will never be able to stop all people from doing reckless things. Nor should we try; in many situations, their actions are none of our beeswax. When such stupid activities endanger others (or us), however, attempting correction is neither impolite (though it must be done graciously) nor something to be entered into lightly.

You may be attending a wedding in a public park, and you may notice people smoking in the shade of a "Fire Danger Very High" warning sign. Do you interfere, in an effort to prevent forest fires? It's almost tempting to wish that a fire would start, just to teach the numbskulls a lesson. But in such a scenario, there is little margin for stupidity, and it would be difficult to enjoy any "I told you so" satisfaction while helicopters rescued you and the rest of the wedding party from a raging forest fire. You don't want to cause any unpleasantness or be a "goody-two-shoes," but valid safety concerns may provide a reason to step in. If you feel that the smokers pose a real danger, you could assume (or pretend to

I'm Gonna Tell!

Never involve yourself in an unpleasant confrontation when you can do something as simple as alerting the proper authorities. When you are faced with a person who is perhaps dangerously antisocial, it is wise to let the law deal with him.

❧ For example, if your lungs are bothered by a smoker behind you in an outdoor movie-theater line, you would be within your rights to politely ask him to put out his cigarette. But if you notice a smoker *in the movie theater,* that smoker is very likely someone with whom you do not want to interact. Unlike the smoker outdoors, he is willfully breaking a familiar rule. He may just respond to your request with serious unpleasantness. So what do you do? Find a movie-theater authority.

❧ Americans generally learn, sometime during childhood, that there is nothing worse than being a "tattle-tale." But the authorities are there to protect and serve you, and most bullies (people who are aggressively rude are just that: bullies) are, at heart, cowards. Cowards can be brought into line by a uniform of just about any kind.

❧ In fact, bullies count on the fact that you won't tell on them, that you will put up with their mistreatment because you cannot do anything about it yourself. Polite people often feel as though they have no recourse when they are terribly mistreated. I exhort you to tattle as necessary. Tattle with gusto.

assume) that they hadn't noticed the rangers' warning. Then you could offer to fetch a cup of water for the cigarette butts.

The smokers will very likely not be grateful for your intercession. Perhaps they won't even respond kindly. But then, good manners help us remain steadily courteous even to people who make a point of expressing their disregard for us—even if the only courtesy they deserve is your cold shoulder.

 ## The Gift that Keeps on Giving

Dear
Social Grace,

What should I say to someone who knowingly exposed me to a sexually transmitted disease? I see this person infrequently, but the city in which I live is really a small town, and we know some of the same people (which is how I know that he knew that he was contagious when we had our encounter). Though this particular STD was easily cured and not life-threatening, I don't think that I'll be able to be pleasant to him when I run into him again.

Dear Cured
Madam or Sir,

As you may know, Social Grace wants you to assume the best of people. If you can do so in this situation—you may have to try *very* hard—your first attempt at conversation would be a telephone call in which you inform this fellow that he may be leaving behind more than pleasant memories and his phone number when he exits a partner's bedroom. There's a chance that he doesn't know (or didn't know then), and if you can believe this, you'll feel much better about the situation.

After that discussion, if you are certain that this cad willfully put your health in danger, you need not be pleasant—or even particularly talkative—when you run into him again. What could you say that would have any effect? He doesn't care about you, and your opinions of his behavior won't change him. I wouldn't waste my breath. He would, however, meet my icy, icy shoulder whenever he came near me.

Should he ever come to you with abject apologies of the crawling-on-the-floor sort and protestations of innocence, you may raise your temperature to frosty. But no matter what, I'd keep a safe distance from this person forevermore.

For the worst of the worst, there is always the cold shoulder. Ignoring someone is quite impolite, but if you have reason to do so, it can be politely applied rudeness. When someone does you grievous harm, you have a very satisfying, noble way to exact your revenge: Cut him dead—when you see him in public, pretend he's invisible. Do not speak to him when you meet. If you must speak to him (if, for example, you are introduced by an unwitting host), a bare-minimum, sternly polite tone and a brief "Hello" make your feelings plainer than even the nastiest outburst, and at the same time, this spares the people around you the embarrassment of a big scene.

For the cold shoulder to work, you *must* keep from saying nasty things about the object of your scorn (of course, you may commiserate with your closest loved ones, but don't slam the scoundrel every time his name comes up in conversation). Otherwise, the nobility and righteousness of your anger is severely compromised. (Being despised hurts. Being despised by someone whom everyone else admires as a paragon of moral rectitude—that *really* hurts.)

These phrases might come in handy: "I don't care to associate with him," "It's nothing that would interest you," and "It's a private matter."

This tack has a sly benefit: What people imagine the scoundrel did is almost certain to be at least as bad—if not worse—than what he did, in fact, do. The most important benefit, though, is that this refusal to engage is a very effective way to keep an untrustworthy, unsavory person out of your life.

You Work Hard for the Money

Workers of the world, unite.
—KARL MARX

Workplace etiquette can be complicated. What constitutes "good manners" is very dependent on circumstances; your behavior at a business meeting will vary depending on whether you are the client or the service provider, a guest or a host, a senior employee or an intern—and none of these business-behavior rules is necessarily appropriate at a social cocktail party. Luckily, we working stiffs are generally a pretty smart bunch, so we shouldn't have too much trouble sorting through these complications. And people who observe the rules of courteous behavior in their working lives are generally more successful than those who do not.

Confusion about the boundary between our professional lives and our social lives is a major source of workplace problems. Though we are increasingly encouraged to think of our coworkers as "family" and "friends," the misuse of such terms is just one of the ways that huge, faceless corporations trick us into working eighteen-hour days, sleeping under our desks, and living on the congealed-oil-and-sawdust treats provided by

Context Counts

Observing all the rules of formal manners can get you in trouble in some situations. Paying attention to context is as important as understanding etiquette's nuances—that is, you should adjust your behavior so it is appropriate to where you are. Insisting on calling the boss "Mr. Grant" when everyone else calls him "Lou" is like insisting on a knife and fork with which to eat your hotdog at a softball game—it looks sort of like good manners, but all it really does is make other people uncomfortable (which is the exact opposite of etiquette's goal). If you're having trouble in a new workplace environment, ask what is expected of employees. For example, ask a hiring manager what your boss likes to be called, or ask how casual the environment is.

hallway vending machines. In fact, sometimes a coworker is just a coworker, and that's okay. A well-mannered person does not reserve courtesy for her friends. Rather, she extends friendly goodwill even to people with whom she is on strictly professional terms. And she begins using her good manners from the moment she meets a colleague, client, or manager.

Often, how to address a coworker or boss is unclear. (Is it "Lou" or "Mr. Grant"?) If you are truly unsure about how to behave in an office situation, it is usually better to err on the side of formality. Before you are invited to call a colleague or a boss by his or her first name, use the last name. In many workplaces, proper etiquette still asks us to call Mr. Powers "Mr. Powers" until he invites us to call him by his given name. (And he is to call you "Ms. Goodworthy.") However, in a casual situation, this bit of well-mannered behavior may not happen—and insisting on formality might make Mr. Powers uncomfortable, brand you as "uptight" (shudder), and potentially cost you a valuable client or job. You can deal with this problem by stating, at the very beginning of a professional relationship (during the first phone call or e-mail), "This is Maybelle" or "Please call me Maybelle." Then wait for Mr. Powers to introduce himself (as he probably will) as "Pablo" before calling him anything.

Although in some places and among some people, old-fashioned, "ladies-first" behavior regarding the treatment of women is appropriate and still in vogue, equal treatment is always correct in the workplace. Indeed, unequal treatment is in many cases illegal. Some people automatically practice social manners at the office—but, for example, a gentleman's racing to a table to hold a woman's chair for her is generally incorrect at a strictly business lunch. (Social Grace understands that there are some situations in which the line between *social* and *business* is very murky.) If they so desire, ladies can greatly help confused gentlemen and set a proper professional tone by saying something like "Please don't get up" if someone does so when she leaves the conference-room table, for example. Here are some more guidelines:

- In your office, the person who reaches the door first should hold it; the person nearest the open elevator should enter it first; and so on. To do otherwise is not a grave faux pas, but there is just no need to make a big fuss over doors in an office building.

- Men and women shake hands with one another.
- When making introductions, the less "honored" person is presented to the more "honored" one. For example, a junior employee should be introduced to a more senior person, a coworker to a guest, and so on.

Truly, if you make gender differences an issue at work, or if you let water-cooler discussion head toward a sex-related topic, you do so at great peril.

Sexual Harassment

Dear
Social Grace,

I work for a small company. It's a fairly informal work environment, and I manage a team of several people. Recently, I was reprimanded by a woman, "Laura," on my team for telling another woman team member, "Jennifer," that she looked nice. Those were my exact words: "Jennifer, you look nice today." Later, Laura took me aside and told me that a comment like that could be construed as sexual harassment, and that it was inappropriate for the workplace.

I know that Laura is right, but I feel that this is political correctness gone too far. When did it become improper to tell a person that he or she looked nice? I certainly don't want to get sued, but I feel that gentlemanly manners are being swept away by asinine new rules about what can and can't be said in the work-

place. My intentions were purely friendly. Isn't there some way I can be a gentleman and not worry about a lawsuit? Do the new etiquette rules require me to be ungentlemanly?

Dear Gentlemanly Sir,
I assume from your letter that you are probably new to the workplace. I welcome you to it. But forgive me if I don't join you in lamenting the end of "old-fashioned gentlemanly behavior" such as commenting on a coworker's looks—because it never existed. Proper etiquette never recommended telling colleagues that they "look nice" at the office. It might've been commonplace, but it wasn't gentlemanly.

The major asininity going on in the workplace today is not political correctness but the creeping informality that causes people to confuse coworkers with friends. I think this misapprehension might be contributing to your inappropriate comments. Women have fought long and hard (and are still fighting) to be treated as equals in the workplace. Sexual harassment is a big problem that causes a lot of suffering, and any hint of it rightly makes people very uneasy. As someone responsible for personnel management, you should be aware of these things. A better way to inspire good feelings on your team would be to compliment your employees on how well they do their jobs.

With an infinite number of conversation topics at your disposal, I don't know why you'd want to risk discussing personal appearance. This topic is a minefield unless you know a person quite well. (And what about your coworkers whose looks don't warrant appreciative comments?) But if your work schedule permits you a discussion with colleagues about the weather, Japanese restaurants, holiday plans, Wagner operas—or whatever—that's marvelous. I'm all for social chitchat. I am, however, uncomfortable with those who take the new informality in the workplace (which I don't deny) to mean that they are invited to treat all colleagues as intimate friends.

Meetings matter. If you must cancel a meeting, do so with as much notice as possible, and if you are going to be more than a few minutes late, telephone. If you know that a meeting will have to end after thirty minutes, letting your guest know that fact when the meeting starts is a good idea. (And always be sensitive to others' attempts to draw meetings to a close.) Saying something like "We're going to have to finish up soon, so I'd like to just sum up what we've discussed" is a good way to end a meeting, and a host can rise to indicate that an appointment is at an end.

Your office e-mail box is another great place to employ smart silence. It's so easy—so terribly, terribly easy—to type out an angry e-mail and send it off without a thought. But before you e-mail that harshly worded missive, wait. If you find yourself struggling to find a phrase that's *really* going to get your correspondent's goat, stop typing immediately. Or write the angry e-mail if you want, but put off sending it for a few days.

You might reconsider your words. The best response to another person's angry e-mail is silence. Before you say anything else, wait until you're not angry anymore. And then consider handling the matter by phone or in person. Away from the false sense of anonymity that e-mail affords, many people become much easier to speak with rationally.

And remember that e-mail can easily be printed, forwarded, and published online, even though it does seem to have a temporary quality. Before you click on Send, make sure that you have said what you truly want to say, and that your e-mail represents you well.

You should approach your job with at least the same goodwill and respect you use (and expect) in your personal life.

- Answer phone calls and e-mails promptly, generally within one working day.

- Keep your personal activities (personal use of your Web connection, for example) to a minimum during work hours.

- Do not complain about your coworkers, boss, or company to anyone—except, maybe, your significant other or very close friends (and even then, be wary—complaining about a work environment tends to make the complainer look like a sucker for putting up with such horrible conditions).

- Say "thank you" whenever possible to people who help you do your job—and be sure to give credit where it is due.

Giving money to charitable causes at the office should be at the employee's discretion. Most people who work in offices have been asked at least once to give to a charity for which another employee, or the company itself, is raising money. Declining to give can sometimes be awkward, but it is not impolite to decline to participate in a fund-raising drive. And you could explain (if you like) that your philanthropic efforts extend to other charities of your choosing. It would be tactless—and not very smart—to criticize the charitable organization in question. Complimenting your firm's philanthropic efforts will certainly make your nonparticipation easier to take. Plus, it seems to me that two parties with humankind's best interests at heart should be able to have a friendly discussion about their individual efforts to save the world without any bad feelings on either side.

Office birthday presents, too, can raise questions of whether, or how much, money to give. Friends and coworkers are two different animals; sometimes, if we are lucky, we have a coworker who is also a friend, but an employer shouldn't force friendship. Office gifts should be handled by the company, and they can correctly be limited to bonuses for well-done jobs. If you feel untoward pressure to chip in for presents to your coworkers, you should discuss the matter with a supervisor or someone in human resources.

Sometimes, the line between business and pleasure must get a bit blurry. It's important, though, to realize that no matter how social things may get, it is wise to use business manners at, for example, an office holiday party, or a job interview at a restaurant. Until you can truly call the people you are socializing with "your dear friends," you should treat them as esteemed colleagues.

 ## The Business Lunch

Dear
Social Grace,

When you're having a business lunch at a restaurant, at what point should the chitchat end and the business begin? Is there an established rule on this? And I know you frown on cell-phone use in restaurants, but is it acceptable to take an important business-related call on a cell phone at a restaurant if I'm having a business meal? (I would never do this if it were a social occasion, but if I'm "working," I sometimes need to be available.)

Dear Dining
Madam or Sir,

Eating together is primarily a social activity, and that amiable socialization can be an important part of a business transaction. (If said transaction is occurring over lunch or dinner at a restaurant, the parties involved almost certainly think that the social aspect is important.) Although there's no firm point at which one must switch the conversation to business, as a general rule, the heavy-duty business talk should wait until the main-course plates have been cleared away. (We rely on the host to steer the conversation in the right direction, and a client should adapt herself to a host's preferences.)

If you must be available for a phone call during a meal, explain that to the other diner(s) before the meal begins, with apologies. Keep your phone in a pocket or in your lap and turn the ringer off. When the call comes, excuse yourself and answer either outside or near the public phones—this being the part of the restaurant set aside for telephone use. It's impolite to exclude dining companions from a conversation at table.

If you're lucky, you will make friends at the office. But personal conversations should be conducted somewhat discreetly (and relatively infrequently) in the workplace. In a professional setting—and I know that most places of business are not very "professional" these days—whispering and giggling in cubicles should be kept to a minimum.

On that note, speaking a foreign language in order to exclude coworkers (or those nearby) in conversation is impolite, but a polyglot society is our reality (and our extreme good fortune). Of course not all conversations are for all ears. Those offended by others' private conversations in an unfamiliar language are hereby advised to stop eavesdropping.

Dress for the position you dream of having. This last bit of workplace advice is not really an etiquette issue—it edges treacherously close to a discussion of fashion, a topic I prefer to let others handle. But any new employee, in almost all work environments, would be wise to note how respected high-level managers dress and emulate them. Certainly, one should dress to impress at work.

You Wear It Well

Fashion is a form of ugliness so intolerable that we have to alter it every six months.
—OSCAR WILDE

lthough I prefer that etiquette not meddle too much in the fickle business of fashion, clothes can communicate respect for the people you are with, for an event you are attending, or for a place you are visiting. Plenty of style experts out there want to tell you exactly what to wear (and one of them just forcibly removed Social Grace's argyle socks from his sock drawer). But there are too many whims of fashion masquerading as etiquette rules, when, really, they are simply matters of personal taste. Here's an example: 20th-century American men have been told by arbiters of style to keep hand jewelry to a minimum. But hand jewelry isn't rude (*people* are rude). If your boyfriend is not using his pinky ring to injure the people he shakes hands with, and if the ring doesn't feature an offensive symbol, then in Social Grace's books, the worst he is guilty of is either flouting convention (a behavior that many people find attractive in a beau) or being unaware of it (and a romantic partner is the perfect person to offer gentle correction). He is not committing a horrible etiquette gaffe.

Where etiquette is concerned, the general rule is that attire should not be offensive or insulting. *Offensive* can mean any number of things, but in most cases, it simply means dressing in a way that's inappropriate to context: a wedding in a cathedral is not an MTV awards show, and it should be plainly evident which is the venue for a dress that displays derriere cleavage.

To avoid being offensive, you can dress in a manner similar to the way others are dressing and in a way that does not shock. People talk about wanting their clothes to stand out, so as to express personality—but dressing in a way that complements a place and the other people in it says *truly* wonderful things about a person's personality.

Clothes can be highly symbolic. Clothing's original purpose—protection from the elements—has become a very minor concern. Clothing rules and rituals serve several purposes. They can show respect for an occasion, person, or place (formal wear at a White House dinner, say, or our culture's elaborate wedding attire), or membership in a community or group. Most people use clothes to tell others who they are (or who they want to be). When Great Aunt Vivian puts away her white shoes in September, she does so as a member of a certain community to which she enjoys belonging. When younger members of the Grace family move to New York, dye their hair pink, and pierce their lips and navels, they are doing the same thing (and although a much different community is involved, the clothing rules can be just as rigid).

 ## A New Take on the "White Shoe" Problem

Dear
Social Grace,

Does the rule of wearing white shoes only between Memorial Day and Labor Day apply to drag queens?

Dear
Gender-Bending
Madam or Sir,

If you would like to make comments about the appropriateness of a drag queen's choice of footwear, you go right ahead. Don't come crying to me when you get smacked. I'm staying the heck out of it. When people don't follow clothing conventions (consciously or unconsciously), they're making a statement about who they are and whether they belong to a certain group. Drag is definitely such a statement—wouldn't you agree? Drag is a costume—meant to startle, amaze, or delight. I might even argue that drag comes under the category of artistic expression. In such a case, I think rules are made to be broken.

 ## Holy Etiquette Problem!

Dear
Social Grace,

The man I love has some facial piercings, which I think look great on him, but I think he should remove them when we go somewhere that is a "dress-up" place or to a wedding. I say that a nose ring is "informal." Do you agree?

Some people with nose rings aren't all that concerned about dressing too informally; others come from cultures in which such a piercing is common—even "formal." If I were the first nose-ring type, I might remove mine for a "dress-up" evening, even if I did so only because a person professing love for me thought it necessary. (You might have more luck presenting your request that way: "You'll be doing it for me, sweetheart, not for society and its stupid rules.")

The propriety of a nose ring depends on who's wearing it, why he's wearing it, and where he's wearing it. Increasingly, people dress informally, and if your gentleman can remember to remove his baseball cap at the theater and otherwise show respect for others, I can't find fault with his attire. Look at the liberties taken with "black-tie" dress at Hollywood award shows, or at the ubiquity of track suits and sneakers. Clothing conventions are, admittedly, always changing—faster and faster. However, you have to pay attention to context as well as to local customs: There are still plenty of places in the world where a nose ring would cause a commotion. (When you two attend that family wedding in rural Tennessee, say, he should consider removing the facial piercings, if only to avoid upstaging the bride.)

When a subject like this comes up, someone (often wearing a silver stud in her eyebrow) will pipe up with concerns about "compromising principles." But jewelry isn't always representative of true principles, and the ability to compromise (and to recognize when to do so) is a hallmark of courtesy. In fact, that ability is a better indicator of a broad-minded, free-thinking person than a facial piercing.

If you're ever in doubt about the appropriate attire for a certain place, find out! Ask a reliable friend, ask the box-office person when you buy tickets, or ask the hostess when you make your restaurant reservation or accept an invitation.

Some things never go out of style. Once you've decided who you want your clothes to say you are, you can do some research into getting the appropriate wardrobe for that person—what Britney Spears wears to a five-star restaurant is not what Madeline Albright wears to the same place, but both of them will at least "look the part." Until then—while you're still a person who looks to etiquette books for tips on how to dress, or if you just want to play it safe for a particular event—you're wise to stick to quiet colors, classic and conservative styles, and minimal jewelry and cosmetics (all of which have the additional advantages of looking good on all sorts of people).

Some specific clothing items are especially important to pay attention to. Hats are one of them. Gentlemen must still remove their hats indoors. Really. Even baseball caps. Hats are heavy-duty clothing items, symbolically speaking—just look at the number of religions that require ritualized covering or uncovering of the head (or hair). People are increasingly unfamiliar with our society's rules governing hats these days, perhaps because far fewer people wear hats on a regular basis, and if they do, they wear baseball caps, which may seem "not to count." The fact is, they *do* count. For this reason, people are unwittingly offending others by wearing hats inappropriately. (And if you're going to offend people, I say that you should do so knowingly and with good reason.)

So here are some general hat-wearing guidelines (head coverings worn as devotional items are of course excepted from rules governing social hat removal; however, a receding hairline does not make a hat a devotional item): Men and boys should remove their hats (and caps) indoors as a sign of respect. Exceptions include sports arenas (though hats are of course removed while standing for a national anthem), health clubs, Orthodox Jewish synagogues, and lobbies of public buildings. Though on the wane, the practice of removing (momentarily) a hat when greeting or taking leave of a woman or an older person is still current in some circles. And hats should be removed during somber ceremonies such as funerals.

Traditionally, women keep their hats on. A baseball cap, though, is not a woman's hat and, even when worn by a woman, should be treated as a man's hat and removed during the national anthem, and in other situations where a man is expected to remove his.

Whatever you wear, make sure that it's clean (and that you are, too). There is a difference between casual and ragged. Clothes, even if they are denim shorts and running shoes, should

Bless You

You're never fully dressed without a handkerchief. People should not only cover their mouths when they cough (or sneeze) but also use a handkerchief or tissue to do so. The Social Grace Center for Disease Control strongly recommends that you all carry your own personal handkerchiefs. They come in handy so often—from muffling sneezes and wiping noses, to waving at departing lovers from a train platform, to acting as temporary tourniquets.

always be clean and look well-pressed. (Anyone who argues that our manners are growing more relaxed should look to our ever-increasing mania for cleanliness. The most proper Victorian lady would seem, to many modern people, too unclean for polite society.) Modern etiquette may allow jeans at the theater (shudder) but it does not allow for dirt or excessively human smells.

What's That Smell?

Dear Social Grace,

Is there a polite way to tell a coworker that he needs to bathe and/or wash his clothes more often? As a scientist, I find that while the vast majority of scientists practice good hygiene and make sure that they smell nice before dealing with people, every once in a while you find someone that seems to have no such notions. Unfortunately, such a person sits next to me. I find myself unable to sit at my desk for longer than a few minutes if the aforementioned person is sitting at his. It's also very distracting to have discussions with this person because I am constantly trying not to breathe through my nose while at the same time attempting not to show any sign of discomfort, lest I give offense. I am certain that this person is not inherently stinky because some days the stench is not there and he is wearing a new set of clothes. I do wish to be polite, and I would almost rather put up with the odor than offend someone I must deal with professionally every day. Please enlighten me with your wise advice.

Dear Scientific Madam or Sir, We may have done away with calling cards and white gloves, but the demands we place on our fellow humans with regards to the way they smell are quite heavy (leading some folks to overcompensate with excessive perfumes)—proof that etiquette never goes away, it just changes.

Although we as a society have come to abhor the smell of an unwashed human body, there is no polite way to tell a coworker that he needs to bathe more often. Only our significant others, parents, doctors, and bosses have the right to comment on the way we smell—and with respect to bosses, only so far as it affects our ability to fulfill our requirements to them. A supervisor or manager can tell an employee that his hygiene needs some attention if that hygiene problem is affecting others' work.

After you speak to your supervisor or manager about the problem, she should then have a private talk with the individual in question and let him know that part of his job is showing up at work clean. A professional setting requires professional behavior, and you are quite right to expect everyone you work with to uphold certain standards.

Before anyone suggests anonymous notes, I'll say that anonymous notes are at best cowardly and at worst threatening: If you can't attach your name to it, perhaps it shouldn't be said at all. An unsigned note addressed to a specific person is appropriate only for secret admirers, credit card companies, and kidnappers demanding ransom.

Fashion is fickle, but good manners are not. When we students of etiquette dress for dinner, fashion should be a secondary concern. Our first concern is always considerate treatment of others.

You Are How You Eat

If my Miss Manners serves me right,
that protrusion from his left cornea is a salad fork.
—AGENT FOX MULDER, **THE X-FILES**
("CLYDE BRUCKMAN'S FINAL REPOSE")

ating together is not only one of the cornerstones of civilization but also a terribly violent activity. Think of the cutting, biting, spearing—and, if you're a meat eater, killing—that accompanies a meal. Much of what we consider good table manners has roots in making sure that nobody gets hurt while we dine together and in actively demonstrating that we mean our dinner companions no harm. A shared meal can be fraught with danger and high tensions. This is one reason it's considered bad manners to gesture with your utensils; they could, if you think about it, double as weapons. (Plus, gesturing with your utensils is a good way to get gravy stains on the wallpaper.)

Nourishing our bodies is only a secondary reason for dining with other people. In many cases, when we eat with friends, business associates, or loved ones at a restaurant, we are doing so for social reasons—food is merely a complement.

If you can keep that in mind, and if you can remember that table manners exist, in large part, so we may eat meals without alarming, disgusting, or amazing the other people at the table, you will not go too terribly far astray. You may choose to eat all your meals at home, with your hands, crouched on the floor in front of *Alf* reruns—and that's your prerogative (if Great Aunt Vivian can't see you, then even she can't disapprove). But sooner or later, there will come a time when you have to dine with people whose opinions of you really matter—who will determine whether you get a second date, your band gets a record contract, your one-woman show gets reviewed in the *New Yorker,* or your new company gets financial backing.

Here are some simple etiquette rules—we'll start with restaurant basics and then cover some table tips and food fundamentals—that will help you maneuver through any meal. (They will also prevent horrible snooty waiters from sneering at you from behind your back. Deep down inside, aren't you—yes, you, Mr. or Ms. Radical Modern Urbanite— aren't you just a *little bit* intimidated by snooty waiters?)

Be on time for restaurant reservations. Without a phone call from the late party, most restaurants will hold a reserved table for fifteen to twenty minutes before giving it away to walk-in guests—and late arrivals might have to wait for a table to open up. Most places have enough "no-call, no-show" guests—with confirmed reservations—that to hold tables on a busy night would cost too much. But running a dining room is an inexact science, and even the neurotically punctual among us will sometimes have to wait for a reserved table. Making a fuss is inappropriate (drinks or an appetizer on the house are generally reserved for extreme problems and waits of longer than thirty minutes).

At a restaurant, the right seating can create the right ambience. One way to determine who sits where in a restaurant is the atmosphere you want to create: If you are a gentleman dining with a lady and hoping to create an old-fashioned "ladies first" atmosphere, the lady (or ladies) should have the better seat(s)—for example, the one that offers a good view of the restaurant. If two people are dining and one person is the guest of the other, the host may choose to put the guest in the better seat.

With larger groups, there are yet more possibilities. If two couples are out to dine and are seated in a booth (if they're male-female couples, ladies should enter first), the couples should sit next to each other—this setup makes conversation easier (each diner can easily make direct eye contact with everyone but his significant other—with whom, presumably, he can communicate without that aid.) At a four-person table with a chair on each side, ladies sit across from their gentlemen. (This just makes playing footsie under the table more interesting.)

The best way to get a food server's attention is silently, by catching his or her eye and signaling with your hand (index finger or first two fingers pointed up). This isn't always possible, of course, so you may also say (in a pleasant tone) "waiter" or "waitress," or ask another restaurant employee to get your server for you. Snapping fingers, shouting, whistling, or waving arms wildly is insulting. Be kind to the people who toil to make your evening at a restaurant pleasant. Curt treatment of food servers is a sure mark of a boor.

A restaurant professional is there to help you. If you are served something you do not know how to eat, don't be afraid to ask your food server, for example, "should this pitcher of cream be poured on top of the dessert?" Trust me, almost all people who work at restaurants do not snicker at earnest questions from people who genuinely want to enjoy their meals properly (the ones inclined to snickering are far too busy doing so at the people who *pretend* to know what they're doing but do not).

 ## Waitressing Woes

Dear Social Grace,

Tonight, while waiting on a couple at dinner, it was brought to my attention that I'd forgotten to bring their drinks. I apologized profusely, but I hoped the couple would understand. When I brought their drinks, the man said to me, "Do I have an accent?" I said, "Yes, you have a lovely accent." (He was English.) He replied, "So then did you understand me when I said, 'WILL YOU BRING MY WIFE A GLASS OF WATER?'"

My response to his inexcusable rudeness (and being a waitress, I have experienced such unspeakable

103

rudeness before) was total shock, and I apologized
again and immediately brought the water. However, I
wished I could have said something that communicat-
ed, "Excuse me, but I didn't wake up and come to work
today to be your personal punching bag."

What do you suggest I should have said to him? I
would love to hear the perfect—yet tasteful—retort.

Dear Madam, I sympathize with your plight. I, too, have served time
behind a long white apron, armed with only a pen, a
corkscrew, and a pepper mill—meager protection against
the occasionally nasty dining public. So I am no stranger
to the sort of behavior you describe. However, there is
nothing I can add to your response that would improve
upon it. You did the right thing: faced rudeness with pro-
fessionalism, retained your dignity, and did your job,
which, like all jobs, has its unpleasant aspects. In the
case of food serving, one of those unpleasant aspects is
dealing with boors.

Meeting sarcasm with more sarcasm (or with a
mighty swing of your pepper mill) is ineffective and usually begets yet more rudeness. In fact, the retorts that
have probably been going through your mind since this
encounter would only have brought you down to this fellow's level—and you wouldn't want that. Unfailing pro-
fessionalism and levelheaded courtesy often defuse
tantrums of the sort you describe. If you're lucky, they
may also leave the guilty party feeling foolish and looking
like a dolt in front of his dinner companions—which, I

think you will agree, is a satisfying result.

Wine is its own food group. In a restaurant, the host chooses a wine or wines that will complement as many of the table's meals as possible, though he may (and often should) ask for suggestions from guests or from the server or wine steward (it is completely appropriate to ask your server for suggestions based on your meal and your price range). If one of the guests, though, prides himself on his wine knowledge or is from a part of the world famous for wine, letting him choose is a flattering gesture.

The food server or wine steward shows you the cork so you can see that it is damp, unbroken, and not crumbly or moldy. (A moldy cork is an indication that you shouldn't abuse your palate by bringing the wine in question anywhere near your face.)

Even if you are not an enophile, you can bluff your way through your tasting duties: place your fingers at the base of your glass and swirl the wine just a little bit (to expose the wine to oxygen, allowing it to "breathe"), lift the glass to your nose and mouth and enjoy its bouquet, and then sip, holding the wine in your mouth for a moment before swallowing. If it tastes all right, say "Thank you" to the food server; then enjoy your meal. A wine glass should not be filled much more than halfway.

Usually, you should wait until everyone is served before you begin eating—but that's not always true. Although it is generally correct to begin eating after everyone has a plate and the hostess or host digs in, when a party at a restaurant numbers more than six people and some are served long before others, it is appropriate for the host to encourage those with plates to begin—and they may do so. If you're at a "hostless" event (such as a group of coworkers taking one coworker out to lunch), a thoughtful guest of honor or other guest can do the encouraging. With a very large party, you can safely begin eating as soon as a handful of diners have their meals. Everyone waiting for one last person to be served only makes that person uncomfortable while everyone else's food gets cold.

Split the check evenly. When a group of friends decides to split the cost of a hostless dinner at a restaurant, each person is responsible only for his portion of the bill. If a bill seems to be evenly split, friends may take the easy way out and divide the bill's total by the number of diners—and that's fine, provided all agree that it's fair. But if that isn't the case, there is nothing impolite about looking over a group's check (making sure to factor in the gratuity) and saying, "OK, it looks as though Marion and I owe $15 each," before passing the bill to the next person. No one should fault you for wanting to pay your fair share.

And if you notice that your meal was considerably more expensive than others' meals, you can prove yourself a person of check-splitting virtue by making sure that you insist on paying *your* fair share before anyone else at the table is forced to make an issue of the check.

Money (including who owes what) can be an awkward subject, and when you find yourself in a situation where you are paying the same amount for your green salad and lemonade as another diner's filet mignon, three cocktails, and two portions of chocolate mousse, you may find it difficult to speak up. But if this problem continues when you dine with certain chums, try clarifying the terms before dinner: "Marion and I would love to come—but just to be sure, we're each paying for our own meals, right?"

When you're organizing a "split-the-check" event, you must make these conditions very clear—"I'm treating dear G. to dinner at Cafe Pricey; would you like to join us?" or "Wouldn't it be fun if we all got together and took G. out to dinner next Saturday?"

Before adding salt or pepper to a dish, taste it. Especially with a home-cooked meal, see if you might be able to enjoy your meal without adding condiments (adding them may seem to imply that the food does not taste good as it was prepared). It is considered impolite to ask a host for a condiment—ketchup, for example—that isn't already on the table.

Keep cell phones, purses, motorcycle helmets, and anything else not connected directly to the meal off of the table during a meal. If you are dining alone, however, you may bring some reading material.

Eat quietly. You'll accomplish this easily by taking small bites and chewing with your mouth closed (this is why your mother told you to take small bites and chew with your mouth closed).

"Foods We Can't and Won't Eat" is one of Social Grace's least-favorite mealtime topics. Discussions of your dietary regimen, your food dislikes, and your negative opinions of others' eating habits should never be brought to the dinner table.

When eating just about anything, prepare one bite at a time. Life can be lived only one day at a time, and a nice dish of steamed clams should be eaten one clam at a time. Your toil with a shellfish fork must be rewarded as you go, and you don't want that broth to get cold before you've had a chance to taste it. Shellfish, steak, dinner rolls, cheese fondue—all are to be consumed in a way that alternates the chore of "bite preparation" with the pleasure of eating. (Many table-manners mavens are especially concerned with dinner rolls—it is considered best not to butter your entire roll at once; instead, tear off bite-size pieces and butter them one at a time as you eat. Toast is an exception to this "bread rule.") Only children begin dinner with their meal already cut into bite-size pieces.

Don't panic if something inedible ends up in your mouth. The occasional inedible morsel, such as a small bone, can be removed from your mouth with a fork or, if you must, your finger (perhaps under cover of napkin). It not only *can* be removed but also *should* be—choking to death at the table is so very unbecoming. You can then leave the offending bite on the edge of your plate, rather than on your napkin (which you may need to use later for its true purpose, wiping your lips or fingers) or the tablecloth—damp food on cloth is just too messy.

If you must excuse yourself from the table, make little fuss. You should not elaborate on your reasons for leaving the table. If you are on your way to the restroom, you really do not have to announce that fact. The best way for a person to excuse himself so he may, make an urgent phone call, sip discreetly from his hip flask, or check his company's plummeting stock price on his personal wireless Internet device is to say, "Please excuse me." He is not obligated to give a detailed report of his planned activities while he is away from the dinner table or conversation. We get the picture: He needs to be alone for a moment—that's all we need or care to know.

It is best not leave a table to smoke until after the main course has been cleared. (That way, no one will be waiting for you to return before eating, if food is served while you're outside.)

Difficult situations must be handled discreetly but directly. Getting spinach in your teeth is nothing to be embarrassed about. It has happened to everyone. And if a sip of water is not enough to remove food from teeth, you should excuse yourself from the table and remove the bothersome particle in the men's room. Picking things from one's teeth is one of those private activities we discussed early on in this book. And of course, if you notice someone with this kind of temporary, immediately correctable, potentially embarrassing problem, it is kind to discreetly let him know.

Silent Bite

Dear
Social Grace,

Sometime in my education, I learned that it was rude to eat while someone was speaking to you during dinner. Since no one else seems to abide by this rule, I am often left with a full plate when my companions have finished their dinners. Am I mistaken or is everyone else?

Dear Hungry
Madam or Sir,

If you're not eating while you're speaking and not eating while someone else is speaking, you're not getting a lot of nutrition out of a social dinner. Etiquette won't force you to wolf down your ravioli while your date is in the restroom—eating with others is supposed to be a social affair. Good conversation enhances the flavor of food. Of course, one should maintain as much eye contact as possible and appear at least as interested in one's dinner companions as in one's meal, but it is not impolite to eat while others are talking. Just remember to take small

 bites in case you're asked a question.

Wipe your lips often. During a meal, as you enjoy whichever beverage you have chosen, be sure to take liquid only into an empty mouth. Refined types will generally dab lips with napkins before touching a glass to them; this helps keep the glass's rim looking clean.

Placing your knife and fork next to each other at the top right of your plate (diagonally, across the edges) is a way of telling the

Cloth Napkins 101

In most situations, you should put your napkin quietly in your lap as soon as you have taken your seat. (An exception can be made in informal restaurants where putting a paper napkin in your lap would mean laying your silverware directly on a table that may not be as clean as you would like.) At "traditional" formal dinners, you wait until the hostess has taken her seat and placed her napkin in her lap; then you follow suit. If you leave the table during the meal, it's best to leave the napkin on your chair or discreetly (no messy spills showing) at the left side of your plate (I tend to prefer the chair). When you have finished eating, you can place your napkin on the left side of your plate, or, if the plate has been removed, in front of you (neither refolded nor crumpled into a ball).

Back at our traditional formal dinner, we're still waiting for the hostess to lay her napkin on the table, because that is our cue that dinner is over. Then we may place our napkins on the table as well. (I speak of "hostesses" because that's the way things worked—traditionally. You're welcome to substitute "host" for "hostess," as the need arises.)

food server that you are finished. Do not push your plate away from you or cover it with your napkin. During your meal, the "resting" position for your utensils is at either side of the plate (each utensil points in toward the center of your plate)—once you have started using a utensil, it does not touch the table again.

That old tip that says you should start with the utensil on the outside and working your way in is a good one. But if you begin using the wrong utensil, don't panic, and don't put it back on the table. Just keep using it if you can. In a simple place setting, the knife (and spoon, if soup is to be served) is on the right, and the fork (or forks) is on the left (the napkin can be to the left of the fork or on the service plate). Dessert silverware will generally be at the top of the plate in a formal place setting.

 ## I Need a Drink

Dear Social Grace,

I recently ate dinner with several colleagues at an awards ceremony. We were packed very tightly at our table, and the person next to me mistakenly picked up my glass of wine and started drinking it. I was unsure how to handle this situation. Should I have informed him of his mistake and asked for his glass? I didn't want to embarrass him, so I just didn't have wine with dinner (and it was a long ceremony). How could I have pointed out his error to him without embarrassing him?

Dear Thirsty Madam or Sir, Exactly how low was this gentleman's threshold of embarrassment? Though I commend your desire to avoid humiliating your dinner companions (something for which we should all strive), I hate to think of anyone forgoing liquid entertainment during a long evening of speechifying. In a similar situation, I might take on some of the blame myself (or, more accurately, blame the close quarters) as a way of diffusing potential embarrassment: "Goodness, our dishes are so close we seem to have mixed up our wineglasses." Or if the prospect of confronting him yourself is too terrifying, you might call upon your food server to correct the problem of your "missing" wineglass.

For the record, readers, your liquids will usually be found above and *slightly to the right* of your plate. Your bread plate will be above and slightly to the left of it:

Liquids, right; solids, left.

Correcting others' table manners is not nice, but there are some ways to do so. Generally speaking, the duties of table-manners correction fall to a person's parents or significant other (or someone similarly intimate). We return here to our etiquette paradox: Telling someone that he has bad manners is, itself, the height of bad manners. So what do you do when you end up dining with someone who eats like a junkyard dog?

113

Elbow Room

Forget what you've heard about keeping your elbows off the table—a strict "no elbows at all" rule is unnecessarily severe. The reason behind the "no elbows" rule is more important than the rule itself. Your Great Aunt Vivian made you keep your elbows off the table so you would learn to sit up straight and hold your silverware correctly. She also wanted you to avoid resting your chin in your hands (always impolite, because it makes you look bored or slouchy), fidgeting with utensils and napkins (impolite because it makes you look impatient or a little bit crazy), and—the worst—playing with your hair (just plain unsanitary). I can't go to a restaurant without seeing perfectly lovely, well-dressed young people flipping and flinging their hair about with wild abandon, making it hard for everyone around them to enjoy their dinners. *You must not groom yourself or even touch your hair at the table.* Aunt Vivian would have had you sitting on your hands right through dessert.

❧ When you're not eating—between courses, say—it is perfectly natural to rest elbows and forearms on the table. Just watch out for the misbehavior elbows on tables can lead to.

Several people have written to Social Grace about the problem of dinner companions "double dipping"—for example, taking a bite out of an egg roll and then putting the bitten end back into the sauce (a practice they are understandably disturbed by). In that situation, you might handle things with a perplexed, "Oh, dear. The server brought only one dish of dipping sauce." Then ask the server for your own sauce. This works well because it gives the dipper the benefit of the doubt (perhaps she was so engrossed in your discussion that she forgot herself), while also demonstrating that putting food one's lips have touched into communal sauce is not nice behavior. Teaching by example is often your best bet when it comes to getting others to eat correctly.

When dealing with a stranger—for instance, someone who is picking pieces of ham, by hand, from a salad bar—you might point out the tongs (ever so sweetly—practice "sweetly" at home before trying it out in public; if you can't manage it, don't attempt it). Or you might simply locate a restaurant employee and ask politely for a new plate of ham to be brought out, explaining (perhaps just loud enough for the offender to hear) that you saw someone putting her fingers in the ham. Dealing directly with "Fingers" is likely to be a lose-lose situation, and it is so hard to enjoy a nice salad after an unpleasant confrontation.

As another example, we'll address a commonly cited table-etiquette problem—dealing with someone who continually reaches across fellow diners in an effort to reach the bread. Try an indirect approach: "Here, Reginald, let me get the bread for you." "I'm sorry, Reginald, did you want the bread? Let me pass it." "Here I am prattling away, and you've been waiting for the bread. I'm sorry; here it is." And so on. You may have to repeat such phrases a few times for results. If they don't have an effect, and if the problem seriously interferes with your ability to enjoy time with Reginald, maybe it's time to rethink the nature of your friendship with him. (Maybe it would be better to spend time doing things that didn't involve food at all.)

But the spirit of good manners involves making allowances for, and being patient with, those who are unable to live up to all of etiquette's demands.

 ## International Incident

*Dear
Social Grace,*

As a European, I was taught to eat with a knife and fork and to keep my hands in sight, wrists at table edge, or elbows on table surface. However, I notice that in this country most Americans have done away with the knife altogether (unless eating, for instance, steak), using instead the fork tines to both spear and cut. We can always identify the Americans at a restaurant by seeing whose left hand droops on their lap, who doesn't use a knife, etc. How can I broach this subject to invitees to my country home this summer without seeming like a vieille école snob? I know most Americans don't even know that their table manners are considered atrociously porcine at best in Europe, but I wanted to save my friends from being snickered and sneered at behind their backs, by teaching them a few table-manner basics. (When in Rome, do as the Romans do.) However, I don't want to offend their robust American pride by pointing out their barnyard animal eating style. Please advise.

Barnyard? Porcine? First things first: I must ask you to refrain from so labeling the table manners of an entire nation, lest you offend *my* robust American pride.

You've observed that some Americans operate utensils differently from some Europeans; however, you seem to believe, erroneously, that one way is better. The "American" style of using a knife and fork (holding a fork in the right hand and switching hands when a knife is required) is perhaps more complicated than what we often call the "Continental" way (holding a fork in the left hand and using a knife to maneuver food onto it), but it is not incorrect—it is, though, rapidly being replaced by the more streamlined, less conservative Continental method. Many Americans have also learned that resting their hands or arms on a table is impolite, and in many situations it is (in some European countries, too), though some consider this rule old-fashioned and severe.

You raise a valid point: Travelers should be aware of proper etiquette in the countries they visit. It's up to them to learn the basics. However, in some cases, asking travelers to adopt all customs is impossible. Some people can't operate chopsticks, say. Some can't comfortably hold forks in their left hands. And some—you, for example—find the way things are done in the countries they visit somehow inferior and decide to disregard them.

Well-mannered people forgive minor table-manner transgressions and differences that occur for reasons of ignorance or foreignness. I won't forgive, however, "snickering and sneering" at anyone—certainly the only "atrocious behavior" you describe in your letter and the only behavior I might attempt to correct in a friend.

Sushi

If you've moved to a city from a small town (and you are not Japanese or Japanese-American), sushi may be a new food to you, and it can present difficulties. A piece of sushi should be eaten whole, if possible, but a piece of sushi too large to be eaten gracefully in one bite can be bitten in half. It is not incorrect to pick up a piece of seaweed-wrapped sushi with the fingers, to make biting easier. (If it's on a shared plate, use the back end of the chopsticks—the part that hasn't touched your mouth—to transport the piece to your dish.) Using a chopstick—or even a knife, if one is available—to cut a piece of unwieldy sushi in half is another acceptable option.

Do not grip your knife in your fist. To do so just looks rather threatening. Hold your knife with your index finger on top, and keep it low—never gesture with your silverware.

Don't fear your food. There are right and wrong ways to eat your dinner, yes, but you can often let common sense be your guide. If a method is messy, unattractive, or dangerous, it's probably incorrect table manners.

Spoon soup away from you. It's just less likely to spill that way. Try to avoid slurping, and when you have finished, put the spoon on the service plate under the bowl (if there is one) instead of in the soup bowl. It is permissible to drink broth soups served in cups, but you would not drink soup served in a low, broad plate.

Yes, Virginia, you can eat asparagus with your fingers. That is, as long as it is not covered in sauce and is not too limp. Crisp bacon, too, is correctly eaten with the fingers. Other finger foods include celery and other types of raw, undressed vegetables, corn on the cob, and olives.

 ## Etiquette on the Half Shell

*Dear
Social Grace,*

I always thought that it was okay to eat oysters with your hands, slurping them right off the shell, but there has been some disagreement on this matter with my squeeze, who doesn't even like oysters but says that eating them this way is crude. I humbly ask for approval from any corner.

Dear Slurping
Madam or Sir,

Oysters on the half shell are usually considered good for a squeezy relationship, and I'm sorry to hear that in your case they've caused something of a rift. Unfortunately, the only approval I can offer you is conditional. Oysters may be eaten from the shell in an informal setting such as a picnic or a casual oyster bar. In a more formal setting, however, one should use a shellfish fork. To do so, hold the shell in one hand, remove the oyster with the fork, and dip it in any available sauce (or use the fork to place a dollop of sauce or horseradish on the oyster before removal). You'll have to use your judgment: If the table is set with linen napkins, you'll probably find the tiny shell-fish fork nearby, in which case you should use it. If there's sawdust on the floor, it's unlikely you'll find—or need—a shellfish fork, in which case slurping is not considered crude (keeping sound levels within decent limits, for course). As you make your way through these murky etiquette waters, though, the most expedient plan of action might be to please your decorum-minded squeeze and use any handy fork.

Difficult food may be more trouble than it's worth. If you're going on a date with a new love or dining with your boss—or even just wearing white silk—you might consider avoiding tricky foods such as game hens and long pasta. (I never order noodles when I am dining with someone I want to impress.) When in doubt about how to eat something, you can keep an eye on your host or look to someone whose table manners you trust. And here are some tricks.

- Most people agree that the following method of eating spaghetti is most elegant: While holding a large spoon in your left hand, almost perpendicular to the dish of pasta, spear a couple of pieces of pasta with the fork in your right hand; then twirl, twirl, twirl with the tines of the fork against the spoon. When the pasta is firmly wound on the fork, lift it to your mouth and eat (leaving the spoon in your hand, resting on the dish).

■ One Asian method of eating noodles served in soups is to keep your face relatively close to the bowl and use chopsticks to maneuver a few noodles at a time into your mouth, step by step. You will need to do some slurping to get the noodles into your mouth this way (still, it does not involve spitting noodles back into the soup). Many people have learned, correctly, that slurping noises are incorrect at Western tables. However, in many Asian cultures, slurping and sipping noises while eating soup are absolutely correct—in fact, encouraged. What does this mean for modern urbanites consuming fusion Asian cuisine at a noodle bar (or in any of myriad foreign-food situations)? Well, it means that they must put at least as much thought into their choice of behavior as into their choice of outfits. For example, there are a number of factors to consider in this situation: How strongly are you affected by your culture's approval or disapproval of slurping? Do you fear your dining partners will be put off by a slurp? Is the restaurant the type of Asian-theme restaurant that is slurp-appropriate? And why not just have the tempura instead? The answers to these and similar mealtime questions will dictate your behavior in all sorts of dining situations, but answering them is no harder than answering "Does this shirt go with these pants?"

■ Crab or lobster served in the shell generally comes with a nutcracker and a seafood fork: use the former to break the shell and the latter to extract meat. Your shellfish fork will generally be the smallest fork in your place setting.

- Game hens and small birds can be picked up in the fingers after as much meat as possible has been removed with a knife and fork. These can be messy, difficult dishes, and only cruel, cruel hostesses serve them unless they know their guests very well, and know that those guests will be comfortable eating them.

- When eating hors d'oeuvres at a party, keep a napkin on hand for greasy fingers, and find somewhere to set your drink down: it is difficult to hold a food item, a drink, and a napkin in only two hands.

- Large, unwieldy pieces of lettuce in a salad *can* be cut with a knife and fork. There is a common myth about that one must not use a knife on salad. While this is a good *kitchen* rule (some knives can discolor lettuce leaves), sometimes there is no alternative at the table.

 ## Ladylike Appetites

Dear
Social Grace,

Is it or is it not polite for a lady to always leave some food on her plate? I was taught this by my mother, but several times recently when I have done this, people have asked me if I didn't like my food. I didn't know what to say.

Dear Ladylike
Madam,

Perhaps your mother and my mother could fight this one out. If my sister Amazing ever left an uneaten morsel on her plate, Mother Grace brought out stories of starving children scattered across the globe who would be "more than happy for some creamed corn," which Amazing was required to completely finish before leaving the table.

Your mother may have been taught by her mother that it was more polite for a lady to leave some of her dinner on her plate. In this way, she would not frighten any men in the room with her wanton display of appetite (considered by some to be strictly a masculine sensation). I'd describe this practice as an etiquette fad (never truly a requirement of polite behavior) that has largely—if not completely—passed out of fashion, to the good of all concerned. In fact, in many cultures, leaving food on a plate might be considered impolite.

Well-mannered women are not required to leave food on their plates, and there are those who would argue that wastefulness solely for appearance's sake is too decadent for words, as those starving children my mother was concerned about still exist in large numbers. If you do choose to leave food on your plate—for whatever reason (whether to seem to exist on sparkling water and Victorian sighs, or to avoid eating undercooked gnocchi that is altogether too gummy to swallow)—that's your business. It's rather unseemly to take too much of an interest in what others are eating or not eating. To stop friends from piling second helpings on your plate, all you need say is, "No, thank you." You can add, as necessary, "It was delicious, but I couldn't eat another bite!" I have a few generous friends to whom this must be said once, twice, or three times, but eventually it does work.

We can't wait for dessert! We are generally given dessert spoons and/or dessert forks. For ice cream, custards, and the like, we use the former. For pie or cake, we use the latter. For pie à la mode and cream-filled pastries, we use the two together if necessary, employing the spoon as an ice cream scoop or as a cutting tool and then conveying food to our mouths with the fork. Unless we're dealing with hard fruit, we rarely want to use a knife on our dessert—doing so might seem to imply that we think our kiwi tartlet is too tough to cut with a fork, an intimation that may very well torment our host for weeks to come. A piece of fruit such as an apple, if served alone, may be cut with a fruit knife and eaten with the fingers. Chocolates and other bite-size treats, too, can be eaten with the fingers.

With table manners, as with every aspect of proper behavior, it's very important to keep context in mind. Even Great Aunt Vivian has been known to eat fried chicken with her fingers. Our sensitivity to others' senses should prevent us from making too much of a mess with our meal at a dinner table—but at a picnic, say, rules are, of course, relaxed (this is why fun foods such as fried chicken and corn on the cob are more often served at picnics than at affairs of state).

Let Me Entertain You

At a dinner party, one should eat wisely but not too well,
and talk well but not too wisely.

—W. SOMERSET MAUGHAM

Any person, no matter how humble his means (or how small his apartment), can become that noble creature—a good host. Since the beginning of history, people from every culture have enjoyed a well-executed party. Indeed, they have likely done so since long before recorded history—even our primate cousins display proper "party" behavior: sharing food with others and getting together for no other reason than to socialize amiably. (However, I hope we can try for more elegant conversation than these distant cousins of ours can manage.)

If you want to be known as "the hostess with the mostest," you must meet one basic requirement when you throw your next party, whether it is cocktails for one hundred or dinner for two: Make sure that you are entertaining for the correct primary reason—namely, that you genuinely want to show your guest(s) a good time. (If you're considering inviting people over for a party because you want presents, you should instead make a list of what you want and then put that list in your checkbook as a reminder to save your money, so you can purchase these things yourself.)

Of course, a modern urbanite may have all sorts of secondary reasons for having people into her home: celebrating the imminent arrival of a loved one's baby, expressing gratitude, making new friends or business contacts, doing a little bit of matchmaking, and so on. But if you cannot find a reason to put your guests' comfort and happiness at the top of your to-do list, you will fail at any other party endeavor, and you should consider renting a movie and spending some time alone that night instead.

First and foremost, plan ahead. For example, make a dinner-preparation schedule, and prepare as much of the food in advance as possible (chopping vegetables, making desserts, and so on). You don't want to leave your guests in the living room for hours while you sweat and struggle in the kitchen. And remember that a party never goes perfectly smoothly. Hosting is a skill that takes a lot of practice, so don't beat yourself up over minor disasters.

Hosts need to make each guest feel at home. Unfortunately for some hosts, this will preclude having quite as much to drink as some guests will, at least early in the evening. When guests arrive, welcome them and take their coats, telling them where those coats can later be found. (And Great Aunt Vivian would be disappointed in me if I forgot to remind you that one never answers the door with a drink in one's hand.) Offer them a beverage of some sort, and give them an idea of where

Hosting Homework

Social Grace has an assignment for those who "can't cook." Of course you can fulfill a social obligation at a restaurant or with a catered meal; however, a gentleperson should be able to turn something edible out of the kitchen when the need arises. If the thought of poaching a salmon for five guests sets your heart racing, proceed as follows:

❧ Go to a bookstore. Buy a good, all-purpose cookbook that gives you instructions for things that other cookbooks assume you already know how to do, such as baking a potato and disassembling a chicken. Then browse around and see if any other cookbooks pique your interest—perhaps one focusing on a certain cuisine. When you get home, peruse your new cookbooks and select a menu. Pretend you are at a restaurant, and pick a meal that you would love to have (with an eye toward ease of preparation—avoid recipes with words you do not understand). Design an entire meal, from start to finish.

❧ Then make that meal. Follow the recipes; go one step at a time. At first you might fail, but do try again. Practice preparing it while at the same time maintaining witty, urbane conversation with imaginary guests in your living room. Make your meal after drinking a couple of glasses of wine (go to a good wine shop and ask which wines would go best with your meal). Make your meal until your roommates, your significant other, or you just cannot eat it anymore. Then have your closest friends over for dinner and make it for them.

❧ Now you can cook something should you need to entertain your boss, or if that hot number you met in Toronto (and when) the evening's entertainment and nourishment will be had. You will have to spend a good portion of your evening making sure empty glasses are filled, gaps in the buffet table are replenished, and all guests are comfortable. Make sure guests are speaking to someone (perform introductions as necessary)—and make sure no one is stuck talking to a difficult conversation partner all night long.

Use place cards. The days of boy-girl-boy-girl seating arrangements at large dinner parties are largely in the past. But if you wish to re-create this era and go with a formal seating chart, use place cards—they can be as simple as folded pieces of plain paper with handwritten names on them. The following rules will guide you: The host sits at one end of the table; the hostess, at the other. The "honor" positions are, for a man, at the hostess's right and, for a woman, at the host's right. Husbands and wives generally do not sit next to each other.

Now, Social Grace is hip to the reality of single-woman hostesses and same-sex couples. And modern etiquette recognizes that they, too, enjoy a bit of formality at a dinner party every now and then. Modifications to a formal seating chart are absolutely allowed, and using common sense to make your dinner party as convivial as it can be (for example, seating two people who have a lot in common next to each other) is always a good idea. A guest of honor might sit opposite a host, for example, and three same-sex couples could be broken up like so:

Hostess

Man from Couple A	Man from Couple C
Woman from Couple B	Man from Couple A
Man from Couple C	Woman from Couple B

Guest of Honor

If you want to be strict about it, it's best to serve from the left and remove from the right. But more important goals when removing plates from a table are not spilling any gravy on the tablecloth, not spilling any gravy on the diners, and keeping the kitty out of the leftovers. If you can manage all of that, you can consider your table-clearing efforts a success. The "serve from this direction, remove from that direction" rule becomes a major issue only when more than one server will be working at a table—in such a case, it's best that the maneuvers are coordinated. Of course, dishes at a diner's far left may be removed from the left if doing otherwise would necessitate passing an arm directly in front of a diner's face.

Feed your guests, but don't force food upon them. Well-mannered guests know that making a fuss over what one cannot (or will not) eat is unseemly, so a host should try not to put a guest in an awkward position by making a fuss over guests who aren't eating a particular dish (even as his heart is sinking because no one has touched the caviar mold). And you should make allowances for guests with dietary restrictions. In most situations, a host who is aware of a guest's severe allergy to peanuts, for example, should try to avoid them. Indeed, whenever a host is unsure of his guests' dietary requirements, he should be prepared to offer something universally edible, such as an undressed vegetable or simple bread. He need not plan an entire menu for one guest out of ten, but he would not want to leave anyone out entirely.

Tabletop Tip

When setting a formal table, put the napkins either on the serving plate or to the far left of the utensils. Many restaurants put the napkin under the silverware, but most etiquette sticklers find this practice incorrect in a private home, as it may require that diners handle utensils before food is on the table.

If a person with dietary restrictions is the guest of honor (or the only guest), customizing the menu would be the gracious thing to do, and foods known to offend should be avoided.

Guests, too, are important threads in the tapestry of a party. Hosts should be good to their guests, and guests have an equal obligation to be polite to their hosts—if not a greater obligation, as they are on the receiving end of a kindness.

Many people who live in cities will often find themselves guests in homes of people they don't know very well (if at all), or at events where they aren't sure what to expect. Knowing a

Quick Cocktail-Party Tips for Hosts

If you are planning large, cocktail-type party, try to put food in one room and drinks in another. This will force people to move about, and if neither of those rooms is the kitchen, it *may* even prevent people from clustering in your kitchen.

~ If you are serving cocktail-party food with toothpicks, position a small dish with one toothpick in it near the food table, before your first guest arrives. This way, guests know where to put their used picks, and you will not find them weeks later buried in your couch cushions. (Similarly, when I serve olives at a cocktail party, I eat the first one myself, so others will see where they can put their pits.) If you must use paper plates and napkins, consider placing a small trash can in an out-of-the-way but easily accessible spot so you can quickly relieve guests of empty plates. (Or place a bussing tray on a small table near the entrance to the kitchen.)

~ If you are hosting a stand-up cocktail party, be sure that the food you are serving can be eaten with one hand. Food that must be eaten with utensils requires a room in which everyone can sit down. And keep plenty of napkins available.

bit of proper guest etiquette can make such events a lot less intimidating. (No matter what the occasion, a guest's first duty is to arrive ready, willing, and able to have a good time—and to arrive *on* time.)

There is no such thing as "fashionably late." Tardiness is not an accessory. I think that people who make lateness a habit will soon find themselves very fashionably all alone in their homes most nights of the week. Anything more than twenty minutes of tardiness requires an apology and a good excuse. (The difficulties of public transportation and parking are poor excuses, since we are all sufficiently aware of such problems and should be taking them into account when planning to go to a dinner party.)

It is hard to imagine that people claiming to be fashionable would have failed to notice that time is extremely valuable to modern urbanites—we increasingly want everything to be fast, fast, fast—and making someone wait is a powerful expression of disregard (saying, in effect, "Your time is less valuable than mine"). If someone told me that repeatedly, I might take him at his word—and refrain from troubling him with further dinner invitations.

Take your seat. At a proper dinner party, no one sits until everyone is present at the table (or until the host urges everyone to take their seats, if he's going to be serving, say). This rule, like many table-etiquette rules, serves to reinforce the notion that, delicious as it may be, food is secondary to enjoying our dinner companions at a social meal.

Whether you're a guest or a host, never make a fuss about what you cannot eat. What you do or don't eat at a party is your concern. Luckily, there is a handy little phrase, which sometimes has to be repeated once or twice, that you can employ when unacceptable food is offered: "No, thank you." However, someone with food allergies or other dietary restrictions may

Turning the Tables

The outdated custom of "table turning" (which, by all reports, died a quiet, peaceful death in an old, quaintly dilapidated Newport mansion) ensured that dinner guests divided their conversation evenly between table partners. It worked this way: The hostess began the meal talking to the man on her right, as did all other women at the table. When the hostess thought dinner was at its midway point, she would wind up her conversation with the man on her right and begin speaking to the man on her left. At this cue, the other women at the table did the same. This way, everyone at the table could participate in conversation during dinner.

∾ Several things have contributed to this practice's demise, one being the wide-scale disappearance of the requirement that there be the same number of women as men at a dinner party. We can also look to our society's relatively new preference for social events that are as unstructured as possible—and this informality is often enforced much more strictly than the formality ever was.

∾ However, we are still required by polite behavior to speak to the people on either side of us during dinner. We are trusted to do that without being forced to. A thoughtful person will be aware of anyone sitting silently nearby and will attempt to draw that person into conversation. And a good host will try to make sure that everyone gets a chance to talk to everyone else at a party.

ask (quietly and discreetly) her hosts whether a dangerous but inconspicuous food is present in a dish.

If your dietary regime precludes eating with others, then that's that. You may need to decline invitations to supper. You might explain your situation to your prospective hosts: "I'd love to come, but I should tell you that I keep kosher /am a vegan/eat no carbs/ have extreme food allergies," or whatever your particular concern is (obviously, this becomes more necessary if you are to be the only guest). After that, you can either offer suggestions

for another, non-food-related activity in which you can all participate, or add that you do not expect your hosts to prepare any special food—you just want them to know so they are not hurt when you avoid the ham at their party.

If you do have dietary restrictions, I suggest that you enjoy an allergen-free/meatless/kosher snack before you go to a dinner where you may not be able to eat. At dinner, you can take a plate of what is offered, choosing (if your conscience and health allow) the tiniest portion of restricted foods, which you can always just push around on your plate. Most of us learned how to do this effectively at a very young age. (Why, by the age of eight I could dispose of an entire plate of peas without eating a single one.) A dinner or party invitation is not an opportunity to dictate a menu. Enjoy the food you can while taking the important sustenance from the evening's conversation. Remember that the primary reason we dine at others' tables is to be social: Feeding ourselves is secondary.

 ## Meat is Murder?

Dear
Social Grace,

Over the years, my partner and I have developed increasingly strict eating habits, and several months ago we dropped our vegetarian diets of many years for vegan diets. Along with the decision to go dairy-free, we decided we would no longer support (or dine at) restaurants that serve meat. Our closest friends of course will continue to tolerate this behavior, but is it fair for us to impose our strict limits on others? How could our limits be laid out so as not to offend new friends and associates?

Dear Vegan
Madam or Sir,

It is most definitely not fair (or polite) to impose your diet on people who invite you to dinner. If you were to invite a meat-eater to dine with you at your favorite vegetarian restaurant, you would not be required to procure a pork chop for her. The reverse is also true, even though your diet may seem to you to be morally or otherwise superior to hers.

In order to avoid offending new friends and associates, "laying out limits" should probably be avoided. It just doesn't sound very friendly, does it? When invited to dine with others at a restaurant that serves meat, you should say something such as, "I'm so sorry we won't be able to join you. Ramona and I do not eat in restaurants that serve meat. Perhaps we can join you later in the evening or another time." The hostess may choose to accommodate you by changing her plans; she may not. It's up to her. Of course, if you are doing the hosting, you may choose a restaurant that you like.

Guests should help out. A good guest arrives prepared to have a good time (even if doing so will require a little work). She makes every effort to socialize with other guests, introducing herself if the host cannot introduce her. She will even have some topical subjects at the ready. But her activities in that area shouldn't usurp the host's role. It is possible to overdo it, and if you find yourself standing atop a coffee table and exhorting people to reveal their most-embarrassing moments, you may have gone too far.

With respect to physical labor, a good guest offers to help clean up after a dinner but *does not* press the issue if that offer is declined.

Down, Boy

Dear
Social Grace,

When one leaves the bathroom, should the toilet lid be left down, which seems more delicate, or up, which seems more inviting?

Dear Inviting
Madam or Sir,

A toilet is, by its nature, already just as inviting as it needs to be. When I was young, Mother Grace (who, like most mothers, understood the bathroom's additional role as occasional sanctuary) insisted that the commode be closed when not in use. She wanted mainly to prevent the dog from drinking out of the basin, it's true, but this simple rule seems a good one even in petless homes, for reasons I'm sure I need not elaborate here.

The guest who stays overnight has a few additional obligations. Hosts who have made plans for overnight guests know that quite a bit of work is involved, no matter how much they are looking forward to the occasion. A guest can show his appreciation by doing the following:

- A good guest either brings a host gift or purchases something during the stay, even if that something is just dinner for his hosts. A host gift shouldn't be extravagant; you might bring something from your city that's hard for your hosts to get (for example, a San Franciscan might bring Napa Valley wine). You might also keep your eyes and ears open during your stay and figure out the perfect gift while you are there, but many people prefer not to arrive empty-handed.

- A good guest is complimentary ("You've done such a wonderful job with your apartment!") and easygoing ("I'm sure that any restaurant you like will be just fine!"), and he complies with his hosts' schedules as much as possible. If you're staying for more than a couple of days, you may try to find a way to give your hosts some private time, even if it is just by visiting a museum on your own one afternoon or taking in a movie one evening.

- A good guest cleans up after himself. As a kindness to hosts, you should strip the guestroom bed (or living-room sofa, if that's where you've been sleeping), tidy up the bedspread, loosely fold the used linens, and leave them in a pile at the foot of the bed. This way, the sheets will not be overlooked on laundry day (dirty sheets hidden in a made-up bed might be forgotten until another guest arrives). The bed should look neat enough that an exhausted host can leave the guestroom alone for a couple of days while he recovers from your visit. The same goes for towels—a pile in the bathroom is fine (but it should be a pile of folded towels).

Accidents will occur. You need not cry over spilt marinara sauce. Say you are a guest in someone's home, and you spill some marinara sauce on your host's exquisite new throw rug. What do you do? Or, conversely, you open your home to a distant relative who accidentally pulverizes the lovely vase you got on your honeymoon in Portugal. How do you handle it?

Situations such as these should play out as follows: The guest reports the damage as soon as possible, practically falling over himself with apologies and promises to repair or replace the damaged items. The host fights back tears, smiles forgivingly, and explains that it does not matter at all. Ignoring this polite denial, the guest insists on doing *something*. The host acquiesces, saying something like "Well, only if it will make you feel better." (For an irreplaceable item, the host may simply accept an apology and leave it at that, reminding himself that *people are more important than possessions*—even the most valuable ones.) Finally, a few days (at most) after the guest leaves, the host will be delighted to receive either a replacement or some token gift of apology, sent in an honest effort to make amends. And everyone will live happily ever after.

If you're a host, you may occasionally find damage—after a party, perhaps—that was not reported. Just so you can go on living in a world that sometimes seems impossibly cruel, you should try to imagine that your dear friends simply had not noticed. Then put it behind you. (Even if you find it very hard to do that, people who run away from a broken vase are not likely to respond well to a confrontation.) You might try to figure out who the culprit is in this sort of scenario by asking guests whether they'd noticed the damage and wondering aloud how and when it could've happened. But you will end up in the same place, silently repeating your mantra about the immateriality of material possessions. Some people, though, prove themselves worthy of different levels of hospitality. Friends who elaborately conceal wrongdoing more than once should perhaps not be invited to spend more time in your home.

 ## Pâté Happens

Dear
Social Grace,

Say you're at a party. You're talking to a nice lady in a pale-pink cashmere sweater and eating some delicious mushroom pâté on a cracker. You're not talking with food in your mouth, but you happen to have something very important to say about a recent celebrity wedding. So you swallow all your food down and open your mouth to speak; however, as you begin to form words to express your ideas, a very noticeable piece of food—a none-too-small wad of mushroom pâté, cracker, and saliva, all mashed up and goopy—comes shooting out of your mouth and lands on this nice lady's pretty sweater. You and she both notice it, but you're both so embarrassed that nobody says anything. This happened to me.

If you were to spit a big wad of something onto someone's sweater, how would you handle it?

Dear
Embarrassed
Madam or Sir,

I would apologize sincerely without making a big fuss, offer a napkin with which to remove the offending food matter, and somehow endeavor to get on with my life. I might cringe at the memory of this event for a couple of weeks, but let's face it: Pâté happens. Embarrassing accidents such as this—although we may feel as though the world will end when they occur—can and should be acknowledged and dealt with. How are you to continue a comfortable conversation with a big, goopy wad just hanging there like an awkward question that no one will answer?

A host should be able to let guests know that a party is over. I prefer to avoid the transparent subterfuge recommended by many party mavens—the yawning and conspicuous remarking on the lateness of the hour. A little bit of directness, with a positive spin, is often a better way to go

Start wrapping things up at least thirty minutes before you want to slip into your sweats and start cleaning up (or just slip into bed—Social Grace won't mind if you leave the dishes until tomorrow). And keep it upbeat. For example, you could say something like this to each guest: "I want to thank you for coming. This has been so much fun. We'll have to do this again very soon." You can even be a bit firmer than that if the hint isn't taken: "I can't believe that it's almost time to wrap things up! I was having so much fun talking with you all. I'm going to have to throw an Arbor Day party every year." Another great way to hint that a cocktail party will be ending soon is to start serving coffee.

And, guests, don't be that dreaded creature, the party guest who didn't realize it was time to go home. Try not to be the last guest to leave (unless you know you're welcome). If an invitation gives a party's "end" time, note it and try to stick to it.

Inviting Behavior

*Friends and good manners will carry you
where money won't go.*

—MARGARET WALKER

When people think of "etiquette," the image that often comes to their minds is a creamy envelope bristling with calligraphy: an invitation. And invitations are important business: they are social contracts, promises of hospitality. Judging from the letters Social Grace receives, even people with little regard for other social niceties are desperately worried about getting invitations "wrong." The good news is that they really are not all that difficult.

But while people are obsessing about their penmanship, they are, often unwittingly, committing other invitation-etiquette errors. Most importantly, an invitation must tell people four things: where, when, and why the event is happening, as well as who the host is (with contact information).

A formal invitation has a traditional form, is generally handwritten or engraved, and should read something like this:

Madeleine Maraschino and Stanwood Viola [who]
request the pleasure of Matthew Apollo's company
at dinner [why]
on Saturday, July fourteenth,
at seven o'clock [when]
147 Social Grace Avenue [where]
RSVP
555-0000

There are of course variations on this form. To make an invitation less formal, you can change "Request the pleasure of your company" to "invite you to." On a less-formal invitation, you can eschew the third-person forms (replacing "Matthew Apollo" with a simpler "you," for example), you needn't spell out the time (with "o'clock"), and you can use abbreviations in the address.

Extend invitations as far in advance as possible. "Save-the-date" cards are permissible for events, such as weddings, that will be held several months in the future.

Match the invitation to the event. You don't need to call in the calligraphers unless you are hosting a wedding or an extremely formal affair (and even then, neat handwriting will generally suffice); in most cases, a handwritten note on nice stationery or even a phone call will do (the telephone has long been an acceptable way to invite people to an informal dinner party). While Great Aunt Vivian does not like to receive the preprinted invitation cards you buy at the store, most people think they are just fine, and I do, too. In many situations ("come-one-come-all" or "keg-in-the-bathtub" affairs), even an e-mail invitation is perfectly acceptable (though they should be avoided unless you know that your invitees are accustomed to them). Feel free to get creative. As with thank-you notes, there are rules to follow—but as long as you've included essential information, most people are pleased to get any invitations at all (that is, invitations that do not include requests for cash).

Unless you are hosting a fundraiser, never mention gifts in an invitation. It is always wrong to include registry information or gift

The Subjunctive Case

You may notice that, in matters of both written and verbal communication, more formality is implied, in English, by using grammatical forms that give a little bit of distance. In invitations, referring to yourself in the third person (instead of the first) implies formality. Formal language also makes use of the subjunctive case (moving verb tenses back in time) to add formality—compare "**May** I help you?" with "**Might** I be of assistance?" and "**I'll [I will] have** an iced tea" with "**I'd [I would]** like an iced tea." Being able to spot these indicators on invitations will help you determine the formality of the event—and knowing that will help you figure out what to wear.

lists in any sort of invitation. Always. (For one, that sort of thing *really* bothers a lot of people—because it can seem unspeakably greedy.) If a guest is interested in this information, he can ask when he responds the invitation. Requesting no gifts is not as completely unacceptable as asking for, say, cash gifts (this really happens, all the time, according to the letters Social Grace receives). However, "No gifts, please" on an invitation just sounds rather negative (you should avoid all prohibitive statements in your invitations—they just aren't very welcoming), and it seems to presuppose that gifts would otherwise be forthcoming. You might try for something like "Your love and friendship are the only gifts I desire" if you feel that you must ask people not to bring gifts. (When you receive an invitation that specifically asks that no gifts be brought, you should comply.) But it's generally much better to pass gift information along informally if you can, and any gift received should be accepted as a delightful surprise.

When you receive an invitation that includes gift information, you can do the sender a favor and pretend you didn't notice.

 ## Greedy!

Dear
Social Grace,

My cousin is going to be married this winter. In the invitation to their engagement party was a little piece of paper, about the size of a bookmark, titled "George and Elaine's List." I have changed their names to protect my cousin, who had nothing to do with this list, I'm sure. On it is a list of items, including their china pattern, miscellaneous items that they need (like a DVD player), the color schemes in their home, a couple of stores (where I guess they are registered), and their taste in décor.

Now, aside from the fact that I know this is not my cousin's doing but his soon-to-be wife's (my cousin isn't the kind of guy who really thinks much about "décor"), and aside from the fact that my mother and I have already agreed that this is extremely tacky, what do you actually do when you receive such a list from a family member you happen to love? Should we pitch in and buy them a DVD player? And are we crazy, or is it weird to bring presents to an engagement party?

Dear Not-So-Crazy Madam or Sir, Engagement parties—being small, intimate affairs attended by people who will certainly be invited to the wedding itself—are not traditionally gift-giving affairs. In fact, at many such gatherings I've attended, the engagement announcement has been a surprise. Such celebrations are (please permit me an exasperated sigh here) happy occasions at which two people in love bask in their families' and friends' delight and warm wishes.

Now, when a beloved cousin commits a grotesque social gaffe (and that's what we're dealing with here), you can do him the immense favor of pretending not to have noticed. It's very easy to misplace bookmark-sized pieces of paper. File away the knowledge that George and Elaine's living room is orange and taupe until it's time to select a wedding present. In the meantime, try to work through any resentment you're feeling, because the one thing you must bring to an engagement party is a joyful attitude.

In addition to telling a guest when and where a party is, a thoughtful host may provide some other essential information. For example, an invitation can give directions (or even clues) about what to wear and what an evening's entertainment will be.

 ## What to Wear, What to Wear?

Dear
Social Grace,

If I'm throwing a holiday party, is it rude of me to ask people to dress a certain way? I know I've seen this done, but it almost seems kind of bossy. For my party, I want people to "dress up."

Dear
Dressing-Up
Madam or Sir,

Giving guests attire guidelines in an invitation is not at all "bossy." In fact, it's downright helpful. Most people want to be told how to dress, and those who don't will ignore your suggestion anyway. Haven't you ever panicked over what to wear to a party? I know I've spent valuable minutes surveying my closet for the right mixture of casual, formal, and festive, not quite sure what the hosts had in mind—and that's time I could've spent writing thank-you notes or polishing the silver. Granted, invitations themselves offer important clues: An engraved, hand-delivered invitation should have you reaching for your bugle beads and black ties, whereas a photocopied flier slipped under your windshield wiper probably indicates that anything goes. If by "dress up" you mean evening clothes, suggest "formal attire." If you simply want guests to eschew jeans and sneakers for one night, suggest "semiformal" or the somewhat vaguer "festive."

147

Respond to most invitations within a week of receiving one.
You *must* respond to invitations that ask you to (*RSVP* stands
for "*Répondez s'il vous plaît,*" or "please respond." This basic,
practical courtesy is not out of date, and it never will be—in
part because hosts will always need to know how many people
are coming to their parties. How else can they be sure they've
got enough wine coolers and pigs-in-a-blanket? Even if an invitation does not include the acronym *RSVP,* a response is often
a good idea (so you let your hosts know that you have received
an invitation). In response to a formal invitation, the best
response is a formal, handwritten reply (as in the following
example)—but most modern hosts are so desperate for RSVPs
of any kind that almost no one will fault you for a simple telephone call.

Matthew Apollo
regrets that
because of a business engagement
he is unable to accept
Madeleine Maraschino and Stanwood Viola's
kind invitation to dinner
on July fourteenth.

**An invitation is meant only for the person or persons to whom
it is addressed.** (One of those people may be "Guest.") If the
party is an intimate special occasion or a formal event, it is
inappropriate to even ask to invite an extra guest. The same
goes for dinner parties—you don't really want to ask a host to

stuff another pork chop or drag an extra chair in off the patio, especially at the last minute. Depending on the occasion and the host (for instance, a host who is a very close friend may be an exception), however, you might ask when the invitation is made, or you could "hide" the request when you respond: "I'd love to come to dinner, but my cousin Aristotle is visiting that weekend—so I'm not sure . . ." leaving it up to your host. If you're going to a casual, cocktail-type party or a picnic, say, asking to bring a friend is often fine. When you ask, gracefully give the hostess a chance to say no without seeming inhospitable; you could begin by saying something like "I would completely understand if you can't add another guest." Remember that her guest list may have been painstakingly put together. And you should always discuss such an invitation with your host before extending it to your friend.

Unescorted Lady

Dear
Social Grace,

I have been invited to the wedding of a couple I know well. The invitation came addressed to me only, and the invite says, "John and Mary request the honor of your presence ...." The reply card says, "The favor of your reply ... Name(s)_____."

This seems to mean that only I am invited. Now, these two know that I am dating someone quite seriously, and besides that an ex-boyfriend will also be present. I would enjoy myself much more if my boyfriend could be there.

So, would it be petty of me to decline to go on the basis that I don't want to go unescorted? It would be beyond tacky to call and ask if my boyfriend could come too, right? Am I being childish? What should I do?

Dear Unescorted Madam, Only people named on an invitation are invited to a wedding. It wouldn't be tacky to ask whether your boyfriend were also invited, if you were truly confused about the matter. However, it doesn't seem that you are, and unless you handle it delicately, your question might be seen as pressure to add him to the guest list—pressure that may be met with resistance.

I agree with you to a point: Yes, people who operate socially as a couple must be invited together to weddings and the like. And in the not-too-distant past, it was considered unacceptable to invite a single woman anywhere without giving her the option of an escort.

But let's try to see this from John and Mary's point of view: Perhaps budgetary concerns require that they invite only their closest friends and relations. Or perhaps your friends have underestimated your relationship with your boyfriend. (I'd be forgiving of such a slip, and sometime in the future, perhaps, I'd mention how serious my new relationship had become.)

Not wanting to attend an event unescorted is a valid reason to decline an invitation (as is not wanting to run into an ex). Why not attend the wedding, wish John and Mary your best, and tell them that your boyfriend sends his regards? Then head home as soon as it is socially graceful, and spend the evening in your boyfriend's arms, cuddling. See? Everyone's happy. Nine out of ten boyfriends will tell you that they really *don't* need to go to another "friends of my girlfriend's" wedding this year anyway.

A final note on invitations: Once you've accepted (or declined) an invitation, you're committed. Once you've said you'll attend a dinner party, say, only a genuine emergency is reason enough to back out. (Of course, lying is another option—not one I recommend, but we all make our deals with the devil.)

It's the Thought that Counts

It is more blessed to give than to receive.
—THE BIBLE [NEW TESTAMENT, ACTS OF THE APOSTLES, 20: 35]

One reason you may find it better to give than to receive is that when you give a gift, you do not have to send a thank-you note (an activity that many people seem to detest mightily, for reasons I cannot fathom). The trouble is, many people don't seem to realize that receiving a gift is also a blessing (you are sure to have met one or two of them): It transports them right back to a pouty, childlike state in which they expect to get exactly what they want—right now! As adults, we must remember we are not entitled to *any* gift that we happen to receive. So you're getting married? Well, that's lovely, and *mazel tov*—but the only thing you're *entitled* to gain by marriage is a spouse. Everything else is a delightful "extra" and should be treated as such.

Every gift you do receive should be treated as a delightful surprise—the tangible result of another person spending time thinking about you. Not every gift will be perfect—but then again, one should not wait for perfection to arrive in a gift package. One should be looking for it for oneself.

That said, there are some occasions where giving a gift is traditional and expected. The good news is that although we must try to select a gift that the recipient will appreciate, a gift does not have to be expensive (expense is often what makes gift-givers panic) to be lovely. You may give someone a gift of your time, for example, or share special skills that you have. You can be flat broke and still give a gift that will be cherished.

With respect to a traditional gift-giving event, even then, gifts are rarely an absolute must. But, for example, you should consider declining a wedding invitation if the thought of buying or preparing even a token gift for the couple inspires dread or resentment.

People generally bring gifts to showers (bridal, baby, and other) and weddings. In those cases, the discussion of gifts usually comes up when a guest RSVPs or otherwise speaks to the person who is throwing the shower (you should never throw a shower for yourself) or someone in the family (in the case of a wedding). At that point, the hostess (or whoever) can say either "She's registered at Pottery Barn Kids" or "They say they don't want any gifts, but just between you and me, I know they would love a subscription to *The Economist*."

 ## The Shower of the Future

Dear
Social Grace,

A longtime friend has recently announced that he is having a sex-change operation. Another friend has this week sent an invitation to a "shower" for this friend. Although I can't attend, I would like your help in choos-

ing an appropriate gift (if the situation isn't too shocking for you). Needless to say, there aren't any pre-printed cards for such an occasion, and I'm struggling for the correct sentiment.

Dear Struggling Madam or Sir,

Shocked? Yes, I'm shocked—and amazed that someone hasn't already cornered this potentially lucrative greeting-card market. Perhaps some enterprising copywriter will move to fill the niche. As for finding the correct sentiment, I don't think you could do better than a common standard shower sentiment: "Congratulations." You should be able to find a pre-printed card that says something along those lines, but a short note you wrote yourself will be even more appreciated.

Showers are thrown by a person's friends or family to help that person adjust to a new life situation, so nothing about the idea of a gender-transitioning shower sounds too shocking to me. It seems like a reasonably sensible adaptation of an old tradition to modern circumstances. At a baby shower we give gifts that a new family might need; at a bridal shower, gifts for a newly married woman. Combining what you know about shower gifts and what you know about your friend, you should be able to come up with an appropriate present. A gift certificate for a spa-type makeover springs immediately to my mind.

Expressing a preference for cash gifts is a ghastly, greedy breach of etiquette. It also just doesn't make very good sense (make your loved ones resent you, and just *see* how many presents you get). The practice of registering for wedding gifts is not—as many people seem to believe—a way of handing loved ones a shopping list—so asking for money isn't an acceptable alternative to registering. Registering is done as a favor to help people choose a gift, but they may ignore the list if they don't need that assistance.

There is no such thing as a "wedding-gift" price minimum. Any sort of wedding-

Gift-Giving Tip

If you're buying a gift certificate to a salon or spa, or some other place at which tipping is normal, include the tip in your gift. The recipient of the gift may add an additional tip if he chooses, but it's always a good idea to give gifts that don't have any "hidden" costs. When you buy the gift certificate, ask to include an appropriate tip, and make sure the gift certificate notes that a gratuity has already been paid.

gift equation you might have heard about (for example, the price of the gift should equal the price of the meal served at the reception, minus ten dollars for every 100 miles traveled, plus five dollars for every year you've known the bride and groom) is utter nonsense. *It is the thought that counts.*

An announcement (of a wedding or a birth, for example) is not a notification that a gift is expected. When you receive one, of course, you may buy a gift if you are so moved. But the appropriate response to such an announcement is simply a communication of your good wishes.

Making a House a Home

A housewarming party is an odd bird in that, yes, people traditionally bring gifts, but people usually throw the parties for themselves, so there's no intermediary to ask about gifts. However, a housewarming present should generally be a token gift, nothing fancy—it need not be expensive: flowers and wine are both fine ideas, as is a small houseplant or something else a bit more permanent. Some housewarming gifts that even Great Aunt Vivien would be delighted to receive include a small emergency-preparedness kit, a hand-embroidered pillow, and a gift certificate for her new neighborhood's Chinese takeout restaurant.

Isn't the fact that you've lived another year gift enough? I wish I could say that no one throws a party for himself because he wants people to bring him gifts—but I would be lying. But with, for example, a birthday party a friend is throwing for herself, the fact that she is throwing a party should have little bearing on your decision to buy her a gift—although a little something extra might be nice as a "thank you for entertaining me." Birthday gifts are at the discretion of the giver.

A guest should bring a gift in some situations. Host gifts are traditionally brought by guests who plan to stay overnight or longer. It is also acceptable to send a gift after your visit, if that makes more sense. While it may not be expected, bringing a gift to a dinner party is also often a smart thing to do. Wine has become a popular host gift for such an occasion; however, edible or drinkable items are sometimes considered unwise choices for a dinner party, since they can be awkward for a host who has planned a menu and may not know whether to share your gift with other guests. Flowers, a more European-style host gift, are a popular choice, too, but you should first consider whether flowers will present more of a problem for a host who may be very busy with his guests (or who may not have space for flowers if he's already decorated his apartment for a special occasion). Consider bringing them in a vase.

Many modern urbanites travel in social circles where it is expected that guests will bring a bottle of liquor to a cocktail party. Strictly speaking, a host should not expect a party guest to bring anything and should plan to provide every guest with at least two or three drinks (generally, a good cocktail party will let guests choose from at least one "fancy" cocktail, a couple of mixed drinks, wine and/or beer, and a couple of soft drinks). But if that "two or three drinks" thing does not sound at all familiar, if you socialize with more than one person in a rock band, or if the police broke up your last party, a bottle of something might be an appropriate contribution.

Good Gifts

A perfect gift for many occasions is a box of nice stationery or note paper with envelopes, along with appropriate stamps.

Hosts need not display or share gifts that are brought to parties. It has become something of a tradition in certain circles for guests to bring a bottle of wine to a dinner party. As modern traditions go, this is a pretty good one. But as recently as 30 years ago, some etiquette books suggested that the bringing of edibles and drinkables to dinner parties was not to be done—for one, because it put hosts in the awkward position of not knowing whether to share the gifts.

Good guests understand that a host's wine choice may have been carefully considered, and they recognize that providing food and drink for guests is the host's responsibility and privilege. If a guest brings you wine as a gift, you may serve it or stash it, as you prefer (of course, after thanking him). A potluck dinner is, strictly speaking, a hostless event, so the above rules don't necessarily apply.

A gift graciously given must be graciously received. I understand that this will sometimes be difficult.

 ## Terribly Gifted

Dear
Social Grace,

A good friend of my partner is on our guest list for the handful of large parties we give each year. This "good friend" always arrives with an elaborate host gift. At a year-end party, he arrived with a homemade gingerbread house that could easily have housed a beagle or other small creature. The table had to be vacated of food to accommodate it in a "place of honor." The stench from the circular lawn of pine needles conflicted with every dish, and cleanup was horrible. An enormous wreath was presented to us weeks earlier at another gathering, with the request to replace the existing wreath on our door with this ghastly monstrosity.

Our invitations clearly indicate that guests shouldn't bring anything to our home other than themselves. Yes, we use the tired phrase "your present is your presence." Still, at every party we throw, our smallish home inevitably becomes the showplace for yet another gargantuan, tacky creation. I once told the guest that, while it is kind to bring something, it is not necessary and space limitations make it difficult for us. He responded with how superior his gifts are to what we already have, and how his cooking is based on an extensive culinary ability and should not be taken lightly. My partner says that guests are entitled to bring whatever they wish, and the host is responsible for accepting it graciously. I say that if the guest can't take indirect requests via an invitation, or direct requests from the host, to leave their extended personality at home, then the guest is "off the list." What do you think?

Dear Gifted Madam or Sir, Though a guest should comply with requests from hosts that nothing be brought to a party, your partner is right: A host gift should always be accepted with a show of delight, however false. But the notion that a host gift must be displayed or shared is mistaken. Though opening and sharing a gift (such as a bottle of wine or other consumable item) is a nice thing to do—if the host so chooses—etiquette has always insisted that such presents could be accepted graciously and put away. With the gingerbread house, you would have been quite correct to accept the gift by saying, "Oh, it's just lovely. I'm putting it in the bedroom (in the laundry room, on the fire escape, or wherever) for now, as there's no room on the table. Thank you." If he protests, you'll just have to keep smiling and insisting. "I wouldn't want this to get ruined if someone knocked into the table, and I won't hear another word about it." Don't give in to bullying guests. Remember that you are in your house.

You have tried several ways to deal with this problem, and now you've reached the ultimate solution: keeping the fellow off of future guest lists. Your partner finds this solution a bit harsh, and I, too, would not consider banishing a friend from future dinner parties only for bringing unwanted gifts—even monstrously tacky gifts, and even after a desire for no gifts had been explicitly expressed. (I might be tempted to keep inviting him to my house just to see what sort of horror he would bring next!) I would, however, think about excluding someone who had embarrassed my other guests and me by haranguing me to serve something I hadn't put on the menu—or by insulting my cooking.

You must be gentle when telling someone that you do not want her to get you a gift. And as we've discussed, there is really only so much you can do in an invitation. This problem comes up often for people who are getting married later in life, for example, because they already have all the household items they need. But our loved ones often really *want* to give us gifts. To soften the blow, you might offer an alternative, "We really do prefer not to receive gifts; we have so much already. But Christopher and I would love it if you would have us over for dinner sometime this fall. He's still talking about your vegan lasagna." Or you can recommend a movie outing or a sporting event—you get the idea.

Close family members may not be so easily put off. When asked what sort of wedding gift you'd like, for example, it is not impolite to give broad ideas as to interests or needs, without naming specific items of a specific price. For example, you might say to dear Great Aunt Vivian, who simply cannot *imagine* attending a wedding without bringing her dear niece a gift, "Of course we don't *need* anything, seeing as how we're already combining two households, but we're very excited to enjoy our new garden." A final option is to enlist a close family member who is involved somehow in the wedding to let people know, "unofficially," what your gift preferences are.

Gifts that one hasn't received (or been told to expect) should not be commented upon. Our good manners will prevent us from inquiring, say, "By the way, did you get us a gift? Because if you did, we can't find it." That said, it is correct for a gift-giver to check up on a gift for which he wasn't thanked. If after a few weeks you have not received a note acknowledging the gift you sent to your nephew for his bar mitzvah, you may call your sister to ask, "Did your son receive the thesaurus we sent him?"

When you're faced with a nonreturnable and inappropriate, ill-fitting, or just plain ugly gift, your first concern should be the feelings of the good person who gave it to you. Seeming to reject a present can seem to reject the thoughtfulness of the giver, which you definitely don't want to do. There is more to a gift than meets the eye. When a relative gives you a sweater that is too large and not your color, you must recognize that it is still a symbolic gesture, the result of much thought about you. Returning such a gift might be seen as spurning that gesture. Understanding this should prevent you from asking someone who gives you a gift for a receipt if one is not included. You cannot exchange a gift (or re-gift it) if doing so will somehow insult the giver (by letting her know that the gift was unacceptable to you). But it's true here that what people don't know probably won't hurt them.

"Re-gifting" is a common practice, to be sure. But it can be dangerous. So although etiquette doesn't exactly prohibit it, I'll say this: Re-gift with extreme caution. Do so only if you must, and only if the giver is certain never to find out. Always wait a few weeks if you can. And try to avoid re-gifting within the same social circle. (I've heard plenty of stories about re-gifts making their way, through several pairs of hands, back to the original giver.)

Have I already mentioned that it's the thought that counts? We have all received presents we wish we hadn't, whether for political or other reasons. ("A brown velour track suit? Auntie Viv, you *shouldn't* have.")

When you receive something that you find morally unacceptable (and nonreturnable), the gracious thing to do is express your gratitude, put the item away for a few months, and then donate it to a worthy charity. Your conscience will be clear, and you can truthfully assure the gift-giver that you put her gift to good use.

A Note on Thank-You Notes

I hate ingratitude more in a man
Than lying, vainness, babbling drunkenness,
Or any taint of vice whose strong corruption
Inhabits our frail blood.

—WILLIAM SHAKESPEARE, TWELFTH NIGHT

For reasons that remain mysterious to me, many people seem to hate writing thank-you notes. They are very easy to write. It takes about three minutes to write one. (The average American, who watches four hours of television a day, can complete a wedding's worth of thank-you notes in a couple of days' worth of commercial breaks.) Expressing gratitude should not be seen as an onerous chore, a tedious duty that one does only because one is "supposed to." The fact that you have to write a thank you note means that you—lucky you!—were on the receiving end of a gift or other kindness. You have an opportunity to express, in a time-tested and easily recognizable way, your appreciation. You have a chance to give back to the gift giver, to make him feel good. And by making a gift-giver or host feel appreciated, you enjoy the additional benefit of keeping your name on guest lists and gift lists. And just imagine—a hundred years from now, the biographers looking for artifacts from your life will be absolutely thrilled to find a note written by your hand (and one that shows what a charmingly polite person you were, to boot).

A great many of Social Grace's letters are from people who want to know whether they *have to* write a thank-you note for this or that kindness bestowed upon them: "I got a lovely gift from my cousin. Do I need to write a thank-you note?" or "A family friend took me to dinner when I was visiting Minneapolis. Is a thank-you note really necessary?" The answer is usually yes. If you are wondering whether to send a thank-you note, you probably should. I mean, it couldn't hurt. (And if you're wondering how long you have to send one, you generally have a day or two. But the good news is, time *never runs out*—it is never "too late" to send one.)

 ## Gratitude with Grace

Dear
Social Grace,   *Is it okay to send thank-you notes via e-mail?*

Dear Courteous   It is *okay*, by which I mean "better than nothing." But if
Madam or Sir,   you have reason to send a thank-you note (you lucky
devil), you might want to take the extra dozen seconds
and the extra care, and jot a few words down on a piece
of real paper. E-mail can be so fugitive and temporary.
Imagine a dear friend, years from now, coming across
your thoughtful note in an old shoebox and saying to herself, "What a polite woman that Kiki was—just *look* at

this lovely thank-you note." That probably won't happen if you send an e-mail message.

Of course, our very close friends and family can sometimes be thanked for their thoughtfulness more informally (indeed, a Valentine's Day gift is probably coming from an intimate source whom you might choose to thank another way altogether). And for business purposes, e-mail has become the standard—and for many, preferred—method of communication; most etiquette sticklers see nothing wrong with sending letters of professional gratitude via e-mail.

Thank-you notes are a cinch. Although they should be written by hand, they can also be very short. A thank-you note has four basic ingredients.

- a greeting or salutation
- an expression of gratitude and a specific mention of the thing you are grateful for
- praise for the gift, in a sentence or two that should include a word such as *memorable, lovely, fabulous,* or *cool*—depending on the situation and your natural vocabulary
- a sign-off

> *Dear Auntie Viv,*
>
> *Thank you so much for the crocheted vest. It's just lovely; you have such a playful sense of color. I can't wait for an occasion to wear it. Please give my regards to Uncle Mort; I look forward to seeing you both soon.*
>
> *Love, Terri*

Great Aunt Vivian doesn't much care for preprinted cards that already say "thank you" on them. Not actually writing the words seems to cheapen the sentiment. But as long as you do pen the appropriate words yourself, too, a preprinted card is generally acceptable nowadays.

Business-related thank-you notes, can be sent by e-mail. But a handwritten note can be a very nice touch.

Many people find thank-you notes too stuffy for very intimate friends and relations. But no matter what, you should always let someone know—even if it's by telephone—that a gift mailed to you was received. And pause to consider that very close relationships often get short shrift in these matters; a thank-you note will never do harm, and a loved one may be very touched to receive your sentiments in writing, even if you have thanked her verbally.

If you do send a "thank-you e-mail," you should compose it as if it were a letter (not treat it less formally merely because it doesn't exist in the tangible way that paper does). This holds true for many types of correspondence, and it's a good thing to keep in mind when you are communicating by e-mail.

To the Letter

When you say something, make sure you have said it.
The chances of your having said it are only fair.
—E. B. WHITE

The Internet has been blamed for more than its fair share of societal problems, I think, but it has certainly done significant damage to a grand old art form: the letter. E-mail, instant-messaging programs, and the fact that many of us now have a cell-phone earpiece lodged in our heads for much of the day have driven the U.S. Postal Service to the brink of ruin—and they are slowly bringing pen and paper to the edge of obsolescence. This would be a terrible shame. *"E-mails" to a Young Poet* just doesn't sound like an enjoyable literary experience.

But it is not only twenty-second-century readers who lose out when you do not write proper letters. Everyone does. People still love receiving personal correspondence (and it is a welcome break from the junk mail that fills our mailboxes). Because letters are no longer the norm, their cachet has risen, and these days even intermittent and hasty correspondence can earn you very fond regard.

Some letters must be handwritten. Any time you want your words to carry additional weight, a *handwritten* letter is a good way to go. Letters of condolence and thank-you notes are the most important of the types of letters that should be written by hand. (And people love to receive heartfelt apologies in writing.) Typed or word-processed letters are preferable in business situations—and, of course, they're fine if writing by hand is not physically possible). Many businesses now prefer e-mail to posted mail because e-mail is so much faster, but you should be able to construct a business letter appropriate to your line of work (or your desired line of work), even if it is in e-mail form.

The medium matters. For much informal correspondence, anything goes—stationery with a design on it, greeting cards, and even postcards are all fine. But lined paper is considered a no-no by many people (and it does have rather a school-kid look about it).

If you want to be utterly proper about it, formal correspondence should be written on plain, unlined stationery that is a shade of white or a very pale color, and it should be written in blue or black ink. But the letter's rarity is such that I think most people would be happy to receive one scribbled in red crayon on the back of a bus transfer. These guidelines are good to know if you care about this sort of thing, or perhaps more importantly, in case you ever have to write to the sort of person who cares. If you are ever in doubt about how formal to be, err on the side of formality.

A modern urbanite should have appropriate stationery on hand—many people like personalized stationery (with a monogram, for example)—but I also keep a stack of pretty postcards, prestamped, in my desk drawer. So supplied, you will be ready to dash off a quick, informal note almost any time you need to. Send thank-you notes with reckless abandon.

Even when you're composing an e-mail letter, use a standard letter greeting and everything else that a letter on paper would contain. You may safely do away with some of these niceties when you're e-mailing quick notes to colleagues, and so on, or when you become involved in a lengthy back-and-forth e-mail exchange. But in many business situations, an e-mail should be able to transcend its digital medium.

A letter should include at least four things. Include the date (at the top right or left), a salutation (it's best to use a name—"Dear Madam" or "Dear Sir" is appropriate only when it is impossible to find out what the addressee's name is), a body, and a respectful sign-off, such as "Best regards," "Sincerely yours," or "Madly, deeply, truly yours"—whatever your relationship with the letter's addressee warrants. It goes at the bottom right or, in many business situations, on the left. If your stationery doesn't include your return address, you may want to put it at the bottom of your letter, beneath your signature. In a business letter, this information goes at the top; beneath that, the address of the person you are writing to should be included.

Letters and cards should *not* include some things. Avoid excessive exclamation points, inappropriate capitalization,

Write This Down

Wondering when to write a letter or send a card? The following special times are certainly worthy of being noted in writing:

❧ When you want to offer congratulations (on a new baby, a new home, or even a new job or pet)

❧ When you want to express gratitude (even for something minor)

❧ When you want to profess love ("I love you" looks so beautiful in a loved one's handwriting)

and errors (check your work). In formal writing, avoid abbreviations. Give some thought to your wording—be precise and concise. Pretend that you are writing for the ages, because you may very well be doing so.

Although greeting cards are nice, don't let them speak for you. To show that you *really* care enough to send the very best, add your own words to a greeting card, even if you only repeat what the card has said. For example, after you've let the greeting-card company congratulate the new high-school graduate in your life, jot down your own, specific congratulations.

A letter's envelope is its face; make it look nice. Unless it is business-related, an envelope's address should be handwritten if possible (or engraved, in the case of formal wedding invitations and the like). The return address can go on the back flap (for a formal letter) or on the front, in the upper left corner (for informal and business correspondence). Outside of formal correspondence, return-address stickers are just fine.

Use the appropriate respect titles (Mr., Miss, or Ms., for example) for your addressee. If you use notepaper (or a decorated card) that is folded in half, the note goes in fold first. A card with something on the front should be inserted face up into the envelope (so it shows when the envelope's flap is lifted)—this just makes it prettier.

Thoroughly Modern Mail

Dear Social Grace,

My fiancée and I are addressing our wedding invitations, and we're wondering what the best alternative is to using "Mr. and Mrs. John Smith" [one standard way to treat a married couple's names]. We do not feel comfortable addressing a married woman simply as "Mrs. John Smith."

We have discussed alternatives such as "John and Mary Smith" (but this is perhaps too informal); "Mr. & Mrs. John and Mary Smith" (probably the best); and "Mr. John & Mrs. Mary Smith" (this sounds pretty awkward, I think).

Are there any norms being established for the best alternatives? Do you think using one of these options will be frowned upon by the more traditional guests? Thank you.

Dear Engaged Sir,

There are, in fact, some developing protocols for addressing "modern" wedding invitations (and other letters), and they take into account the disinclination of some people to refer to a woman only by her husband's name.

Luckily, once you've decided that you don't want strictly formal envelopes, your choices multiply. And there are, of course, correct ways to address envelopes to, say, married couples with different last names or unmarried couples.

The first choice is to include both full names on the same line ("Mr. John Smith and Mrs. Mary Smith" or "Dr. Mary Doe and Mr. John Jones"). Another option—leaving out courtesy titles ("John and Mary Smith")—is, as you indicate, very informal, but it's not beyond the realm of proper etiquette. After all, a wedding does not have to be formal to get two people started in their life of wedded bliss.

You may briefly startle a very few guests—that is the risk associated with breaking tradition, and you're taking it knowingly. But there is little to give true offense here, and I would be seriously concerned about the emotional state of someone who actively "frowned upon" any of these options. However, if I knew, for example, that my Aunt Vivian would prefer the more traditional wedding invitation, I might choose to humor her.

A condolence letter or card is another important kindness. As soon as you learn of the death of someone who is important to you—or important to someone important to you—send a short note offering your sympathy, support, and (if it's true) a brief mention of how dear the dead person was to you. Above all other types of correspondence, people hesitate to send these very important letters, often because they feel that they aren't up to the monumental task of appropriately memorializing a person, or because they don't want to intrude on another person's grief. But a condolence letter should do neither of those things. It should be brief and it should offer sympathy, along with some kind words about the person who has died. It should never include "advice" or any hint that anyone is "better off." And religious or spiritual talk should be included only if you are certain that it will be welcomed by the recipient. For example:

> *Dear Keiko,*
>> *I have just heard the very sad news of your father's death. He was a true gentleman, and I will cherish my memories of him. My thoughts and sympathy are with you and your family. Please call me if you need anything at all.*
>> *Sincerely,*
>> *Pilar*

Put apologies in writing, too. A written apology can do reparative miracles. Anytime you err—even mildly—consider a written apology (in addition to a spoken one). The apology is an often neglected way to smooth over embarrassing incidents and unintentional etiquette gaffes, large and small. (Who hasn't had his sleep troubled by an unintentional verbal blunder, for example? The next time you accidentally say the wrong thing, instead of mentally kicking yourself for weeks, *apologize.*)

Like many other effective letters, the letter of apology should be short and sweet. Excessive explanations or excuses greatly weaken an apology. **Being a good correspondent is a mark of true sophistication.** The cultured modern urbanite knows that e-mail has nothing on letters—so you should make sure that you *always* have plenty of stamps.

Tip Top

Tipping is not optional at restaurants, in taxis, and at hotels. In these places, you completely withhold tips only when a maleficent food server or taxi driver has *deliberately* mistreated you in some unforgivable way. (Here is another great example of politely applied rudeness: Withholding a tip is wrong, but when it's warranted, it sends a powerful message. And if you've been a rude, difficult customer from the very start, your withheld tip carries no weight at all.) If you receive service that is simply lackluster or marginally inattentive, it is appropriate to tip the minimum—that is, ten to fifteen percent in a restaurant, for example. Tips are a presupposed part of many people's salaries, and withholding tips for mediocre but acceptable service is both incorrect and morally wrong. I prefer to assume the best of service professionals—for example, that my waiter is preoccupied because his manuscript has been rejected again or because his daughter has pierced her ears without permission. People who work in offices often have less-than-stellar days at work without a noticeable effect on their paychecks. Besides, many of the things that can go wrong with a meal are not under the control of the food server.

If you feel that the service you have received is not what it should have been and you want to tip accordingly, it is best to explain, especially to a manager, why you are dissatisfied. This way, the problem might actually be resolved (and you will not be remembered as just some cheapskate).

Tipping well, however, does not buy your way out of being polite. Many people who work in service professions have told me that being treated with courtesy is as just as important as, if not more important than, a couple of dollars, and having toiled in the service industry, I feel qualified to agree. Many people (you may know one or two of them) suffer from a common manners disorder that I call "IIS," or Imagined Inferiors Syndrome. You would think that the absence of a well-defined class system would have turned the United States into a utopian society of perfect equality. Alas, it turns out that many people *crave* rigid class systems and long for identifiable social inferiors. (That this longing is caused by fears of real inferiority should not be surprising.) So some people resort to income level as a way to mark out a class system. Still others define their inferiors as those who toil in service of the public.

This way of thinking, though, can be unlearned—and it is *easy* to unlearn, because it really makes no sense when you closely examine it. You want a cocktail, and the bartender has the liquor. You need to ring your colleague at the Hilton, and the hotel operator knows the room number. Who is *really* in a superior position? You see how the logic is flawed.

The people whose job it is to *help us through life* so obviously deserve respect and courtesy. So if you witness a friend—or Great Aunt Vivian—being needlessly curt with a food server or sales clerk, simply ask, privately, what horrible offense earned such treatment. You could also describe a situation in which you were treated rudely while serving the public and how you felt. Without accusing anyone of being rude, either of these approaches may start a conversation in which you can help someone else be aware of "unconsciously" impolite behavior.

Modern urbanites often find themselves in situations where they are unsure whether to tip, but there is a good rule they can apply. Outside of obvious tipping zones such as hotels and restaurants, a very broadly stated rule is this: When you purchase a "luxury" personal service, a gratuity is more likely in order. (For example, we tip a food server but not a grocery-store cashier, a manicurist but not a nurse, and a shoeshiner but not a shoe salesperson.) But if you're perplexed, the best way to find out whether tipping is necessary is to *find out.* Ask when you make your salon reservation, or check a guidebook before you head overseas. The information is out there—and I, too, can supply you with some basic tipping tips.

A standard restaurant tip is still fifteen percent of the bill's total, and it is given to the server. If you are in a better-quality restaurant, the expected tip is somewhat higher, about twenty percent, and there may be more people to tip. If you were served by a sommelier, there are a couple of things you should do: First, enjoy the fact that you were probably at a *very* posh establishment, indeed. Then, use the bill's total *without* wine to calculate your food server's tip; the sommelier generally gets about ten percent of the cost of the wine (and more, up to twenty percent, if she was especially helpful in the selection of your wine). You can leave the tip with the steward, the server, or the maître d'.

If a maître d' is especially helpful, you may tip him as much as twenty dollars (but waving money at a maître d' upon arrival at a restaurant, in order to secure a "good" table, usually works only in the movies—and in restaurants that don't really have "good" tables).

Tipping for take-out food is not standard, but it's not wrong, either. And how you handle tip jars is up to you. Tipping is a way of saying thank you—with money. Now most of us are solidly in favor of cash *and* gratitude; however, as far as etiquette is concerned, we are not necessarily obligated to tip for food that we pick up at a take-out counter. Doing so is at the customer's discretion. (We are, however, obligated to say thank you.)

Many employers are taking advantage of Americans' natural generosity—and our fear of appearing "cheap"—by paying their employees less and giving them, instead, what they can manage to collect in the increasingly ubiquitous tip jar. For this reason, I find the tip jar rather unpleasant but hard to resist (I want to help those nice kids who make my cappuccino save for college). And when we apply the "luxury test" to this sort of situation, it seems that a small tip—say, between thirty and fifty cents for a three-dollar latte—is in order for coffee-bar service (more for especially special service). You probably don't need to tip someone simply for ringing up an order and making change, but if you've asked him to prepare an extra-hot triple-shot half-decaf soy hazelnut latte with light foam—and he does so without rolling his eyes—well, fifteen percent does seem about right.

You should tip the person who delivers food to your house at least two or three dollars. Tip more if, for example, he is delivering ten pizzas to your Super Bowl party in the middle of a rainstorm.

In a buffet or a sushi-boat restaurant—where one serves oneself food but is waited on for drinks—tips are generally around ten percent of the total bill. So you tip a bit less than you would tip for full table service unless you make great demands on your server.

At a nightclub, tipping depends on what you are drinking and where you are sitting. Bartenders are customarily tipped one or two dollars for a mixed drink (you tip more for a drink that is complicated or "shaken"). Cocktail servers should get that plus an additional couple of dollars per round—if you are given a table bill (or if you are ordering $300 bottles of champagne), you can tip fifteen to twenty percent. If a doorperson hails you a cab, he gets two or three dollars. Restroom atten-

dants get one dollar or so (more if they help you in some
way—removing lint from your dress or pointing out the trail
of toilet paper attached to your shoe).

**Valet-parking attendants are customarily tipped two to five
dollars.** Five dollars is about right for spendy establishments
and excellent service.

 ## Tipped Over

*Dear
Social Grace,*

*Please help settle an issue between a friend and me
on the subject of tipping cab drivers; he believes we
should, and I believe we shouldn't. I was under the
impression that one tips those in the service industry
(waiters, hairdressers, doormen, etc.), where a range
of customer service, from poor to excellent, would be
provided and rewarded accordingly. But cab drivers
don't seem to provide customer service. Perhaps they
did in ye olde days, when they assisted with baggage
or opened the car doors or did more than just honk
when they arrived at your pickup location, but nowadays they provide no more customer service than a
subway driver. However, my friend says we should tip
cabbies because it's traditional. So are we to throw
money around out of a blind sense of tradition, particularly in these tough economic times? Or should we tip
when provided with a situation where customer service could be rewarded?*

Dear Tipped-Off
Madam or Sir,

Yes, tipping taxi drivers is customary. Because of this
custom, taxi drivers earn considerably less than bus driv-

ers do. They also provide what I consider a very valuable customer service: moving you from Point A to Point B without exposing you to tedious waits under bus shelters and inconvenient routes through high-traffic areas.

As thanks, tip a dollar for a very quick ride, and tip between one and two dollars for a ride that costs between five and ten dollars. When your fare runs higher, tip more: usually fifteen or twenty percent. If a long wait in a traffic jam is not represented by the fare, try to tip accordingly. If a taxi driver provides extraordinary service—opening doors, carrying luggage, or alerting you to a terrifying conspiracy concerning NASA, a fast-food chain, and several prominent local politicians—keep it coming.

Etiquette does not want you to throw money around, especially during tough economic times. That's why etiquette requires that you tip only when luxuries are involved. Riding the bus and shopping at the supermarket are necessities, so we don't ask people to tip bus drivers or Safeway clerks (though we should always say thank you). A taxi ride or a visit to a restaurant is a luxury expense—news, perhaps, to those who have never before experienced lean times. If you're feeling a pinch in the wallet region, I encourage you to consider public transportation.

When you arrive at a hotel, have lots of small bills handy. There will be plenty of people to tip. At most American hotels, a tip of between one and three dollars per day to the housekeeper is standard. The cost of the room is a good gauge—a more

By Definition

Just to set the record straight, *tips* is not short for "To Insure Prompt Service." This is one of those strange etymology urban legends that the Internet breeds (and besides, *ensure* would be more correct). The practice of tipping precedes the English language altogether—the ancient Romans, for example, had ideas about how much to tip a prostitute—and the origins of the word are therefore somewhat murky. Many dictionaries link the word with a nearly defunct *tip* that meant "to lightly touch."

expensive room equals a larger tip (and if there are several messy people in the room, you should tip a bit more). You can also add an additional tip if housekeeping provided some special service. Unless you are at a hotel or a bed-and-breakfast with an obviously small staff, it's best to leave the tip daily, because the housekeeping staff may rotate. If no envelope is provided, leave your tip in one of the hotel envelopes in your room's stationery kit or in a folded piece of paper. Write "Housekeeping" or "Thank you" on it and leave it on your bed, where it is conspicuous and its intended recipient clear.

As at other locales, tip a doorperson two or three dollars if he hails a cab for you. At the sort of hotel where a doorperson holds a door for you each time you enter or exit, you may tip that person a few dollars after you check out. A bell person who carries your bags should generally receive two dollars for as many bags as one person can easily carry; increase the amount (by about one dollar per bag) for more luggage. If a bell person or housekeeper brings something to your room, tip about two dollars. A concierge who assists you by getting you theater tickets or the like gets ten or twenty dollars—of course, extremely hard-to-get theater tickets, for example, will earn more.

These hotel employees earn salaries that presuppose a certain amount of income in gratuities, just as food servers do. (And I'm sure that if hotels did away with tips, the increase in room rates would be much greater than the meager amount we would save in folding money. Besides, isn't it gratifying to directly thank the people who work hard to smooth our travels for us?) The one person you should not tip in a hotel is a hotel manager; if you must deal with her for some reason, or if you deal with a hotel's sales managers or convention planners, a tip is not necessary.

A positive comment card is sometimes even better than a tip. Many hotels and similar establishments have employee-incentive programs based on good service. If someone at a hotel goes far above and beyond the call of duty, please look for a guest comment card to fill with praise, or even write a letter yourself. It could make a big difference in that person's career. Even though you have tipped well, and even though you have said thank you, finding a way to let management know how pleased you are with service you have received is a courteous thing to do (you would certainly let someone know if service had been severely substandard).

Beauty treatments (excluding procedures performed by a doctor) are also luxury services for which a tip is customary. Your hairstylist gets at tip of between ten and twenty percent, as does your manicurist. If you are shampooed by a designated shampoo person (or served by any other auxiliary hair-salon employee), tip him one or two dollars. Every month, Social Grace gets letters from people wondering whether to tip the owners of salon. I find it odd that this minor, and fungible, etiquette rule has so pervaded the American consciousness. The fact is, the "Don't Tip the Owner" rule is something of an etiquette chestnut, and every salon owner is different in this respect. Some charge more than the other stylists at their salons, in lieu of tips. Most, though, accept tips gladly nowadays.

The best thing to do in this situation is to ask the receptionist when you make your appointment: "I'm booked with the owner of the salon; does he accept tips?" (At a smaller salon, without a large staff that includes a receptionist, the owner is much likelier to accept gratuities.)

 ## Think Ink

Dear Social Grace,

Do you tip a tattoo artist?

Dear Tatooed Madam or Sir,

According to the inkers at my friendly neighborhood tattoo parlor, nothing says "Thanks for the lovely tattoo" like cash. And I agree that a tip might be appropriate here. A tattoo is more like a permanent haircut (and you do tip hairstylists) than a cosmetic medical procedure (and you don't tip doctors). And it is obviously a luxury. A service's necessity is one good way to gauge the need for tipping; admittedly, the rules can seem rather arbitrary. In this case, a small tip—say, 10 percent—is not mandatory but will be appreciated.) This is one case where a considerate rebel might do a bit of his own research, perhaps by calling a few tattoo parlors and asking what is customary. Before I gave you my advice, I called a few tattoo parlors to ask the experts.

It is often very wise, in many situations, to ask first whether tipping is correct or appropriate—when you arrange to have a piece of furniture delivered, for example, or when you make an appointment for a massage. Customs can vary greatly. And if someone declines to accept a tip, do not force it on him. he is not being rude if he tells you, politely, that a tip is not necessary.

Just as there are guidelines for when a tip is likely to be necessary, there are a couple of situations in which a tip is probably *not* necessary. You don't often tip people in positions of authority—for example, a ship's captain—or people who are not in true "service" professions: doctors, teachers, and so on. You should also think twice before tipping kind strangers.

 ## The Good Samaritan's Tip

Dear Social Grace,

Last summer, my girlfriend and I were driving through the Navajo Nation (in what we call Arizona), viewing all the amazing mesas and terrible poverty, when my car got stuck in some sand. I flagged down a passing pick-up truck, and the driver quickly pulled over. A Navajo couple helped me without saying a word, the rich white man's (my) new Volkswagen spraying them with sand as they pushed my car.

I thanked them profusely for freeing my car, and I immediately reached in my pocket and pulled out a ten-dollar bill. I said, "Would you like something for your trouble?" and held it out. The man looked at me for a moment and then took the money, and then the couple drove off. I suddenly felt a lot of guilt for this, my throwing money at poor people, even though they helped just to be nice, because people still do that some places. On the other hand, I didn't force them to take the money; I only offered, and they could have refused. Did I do the right thing, or a rude thing, by offering them money for their kindness?

Dear
Guilty Sir,

You and I agree that your ten dollars cheapened this couple's act of kindness—one doesn't generally tip Good Samaritans. That your payment was inappropriate becomes even clearer when we edit out this situation's incidental information, such as the (presumed) financial situation of the people involved. An interaction that could've left you with that delightful "Gosh, people are sure nice" feeling and the helpful couple with that delicious "I did an unselfish good deed" feeling was rendered awkward by the introduction of a little bit of money. But don't be too hard on yourself—you were properly, profusely grateful, and the payment may even have been welcome.

It's unfortunate that heartfelt thanks are often seen as less valuable than a few bucks. But there is some smudgy gray around the edges of your question, and I can imagine situations in which a payment for such help might be acceptable. If your plight had required that the couple give you something with a cash value (like a gas can or a rope), for example, or if someone obviously destitute (carrying a "Will Work for Food" sign) had come to your aid, a handout would have been appropriate. In such cases, though, the subject of payment should be broached before you reach for your wallet; money thrust upon someone is potentially insulting, but the suggestion of payment is easier to rebuff and disregard. Next time, try this: "I'm in your debt; can I repay your kindness in some way? May I perhaps pay you for your time?"

And a Happy New Year. During the holiday season, it is traditional, and appropriate, to give a little something extra to the people who toil all year long to make your life easier—your hairdresser, your apartment building's lobby staff (if you are so blessed), your building's super, and so on. Such gifts can vary widely, and they depend greatly on your means (a small token gift is acceptable if your means are genuinely slim). While you can find holiday-tipping guides pretty much everywhere etiquette is mentioned on the Web, you may also ask your neighbors, for example, what your building's custom is if you are unsure.

Love Should Not Be a Battlefield

Romance is everything.
—GERTRUDE STEIN

In traditional terms, dating is the first step in a journey that will eventually lead to marriage, 2.2 children, and a charming home in the suburbs. But many of us have decided that this will not be our destiny—or if it will, that we will not be following society's sanctioned path to it. For many modern urbanites, gentle suburban bliss is not the goal they have in mind as they pursue their versions of love and romance at bars, at grocery stores, on personals Web sites, and so on. A person who moves to a big city often does so with an eye toward creating a nontraditional love life that's right for him.

In the rush to free ourselves from customs and goals that are not appropriate for us, we have failed to create new formulas that ease the difficult work of establishing bonds with other people. To put it bluntly, we don't know how to date. Our amorous pursuits lead only to heartache. Our sexual adventures leave others feeling used and mistreated. And we despair of ever finding romance, which has been pronounced dead more times than disco.

For better or worse, though, they both live on. And romance's kissing cousin, etiquette, can help you find the happy love life, the happy sex life, or even the happy marriage (or committed partnership) you seek. Social Grace's wish is that you pursue these goals with an eye toward treating everyone with respect—because you really should not hurt the ones you love (or even the ones you barely know).

The advantage of following some traditional ceremonies of dating is that they give two people a common language to use while negotiating both the possibility of a relationship and a potential relationship's boundaries. When operating within the specific, time-tested roles of two people on a date, each person knows how to behave—making interaction less stressful and diminishing the chances of miscommunication. Dating gives two people an opportunity to display themselves at their very best and, before any strings are attached, to decide whether they want to start a relationship of any kind. It is a chance to assess another person's potential desirability—while doing something that you both (it is hoped) will enjoy. Plus, a date is a great way for single people who may not want a relationship to enjoy an evening of companionship.

Here is your first dating-etiquette dictum: A date is a special occasion and should be treated as such. But there are a few other considerations you should keep in mind as you paddle in the dating pool.

Anyone can ask anyone else out on a date. Before the fun can begin, you have to take a deep breath and ask someone to go on a date with you. Traditionally, it has been a man's job to do the asking—but in many cases, we can dispense with this rather antique etiquette rule. It simply left too many women waiting impatiently by telephones and too many men shy about asking a woman to a baseball game she was just dying to attend. And the world at large has noticed that not every dating relationship necessarily even includes a man—so this rule left a large portion of society unrecognized, and it reinforced a false notion that etiquette didn't apply to people whose desires lay in the direction of their own genders. The rules for proposing, accepting, and declining dates outlined here are not gender-specific, but they should be useful as guidelines that will go a long way toward easing shyness and protecting the tender emotions of the people involved.

The most important thing you can do before asking someone out is to brace yourself for rejection. Not everybody will want to spend time with you. Their reasons should not worry you at all. (Since your goal is to find someone who *does* want to spend time with you, try looking at the "non-takers" as a necessary part of the process of elimination.) There are, however, a few ways to improve your chances:

- Plan something special before you ask. Make an evening with you hard to resist. If you know a little bit about the person you are asking out, you can suit the evening to both of your tastes. "I know how much you like Fellini, and I saw that *Juliet of the Spirits* is playing" is a much better bet than "drinks after work sometime."

- Set the date a couple of weeks in advance. You are less likely to get an "I'm busy" as a response.
- No means no. Someone you ask out has no obligation to give you an explanation beyond "I'm sorry, no, but thank you for asking." A rejection should not inspire hard feelings. You are welcome to ask again; however, Social Grace gently suggests a "three strikes" convention in dating. If a person says no three times and does not beg you to ask again (or does not ask you out), you are probably wasting your time, and if you do ask again, your efforts may seem rather frighteningly persistent.

 ## She'll Have What I'm Having

Dear Social Grace,

I endeavor to always be a gentleman; however, I have recently run into questions about the propriety of sending a lady a drink at a bar. First, if said lady is sitting at a bar with a friend, must I buy both ladies a drink? Second, if she accepts the drink, may I then go over and speak to her, or should I wait for her to speak to me? As a side question: Does a smile and a nod count as speaking to me?

Dear Gentlemanly Sir,

When we Grace children reached an age at which we might find ourselves in saloons, Mother Grace rather sternly warned us that to accept a drink from a complete stranger suggested loose morals and easy virtue. (Of course, Mother Grace also believed that chewing gum suggested loose morals and easy virtue, so you may take her warning with a grain of salt.) However, I wonder what is preventing you, my good man, from pushing away from the bar, greeting the woman in question, and ascertaining her need for a drink after a friendly exchange. This course of action—trading names and pleasantries *before* you start plying her with alcohol—seems rather friendlier and more respectful, at the very least. If you are in fact a gentleman about it, there is nothing impolite about striking up a conversation at a bar. Plus, a smile and a nod can mean anything from "Back off, bozo" to "Hello, gorgeous." It's hard to tell from across a dark room. (Note that correctly interpreting even the subtlest "back-off" that comes his way is the mark of a true gentleman.)

Besides, even if someone accepts your offer of a drink, she is obligated only to thank you for it.

I know your intentions are honorable, so why not behave as such? Introduce yourself and then offer her (and her companion—you'll want her on your side) a drink. An added benefit is that if you change your mind about the enterprise once you speak to her (or if she refuses you), you can have that extra drink yourself.

Is it safe to talk to strangers? And almost as importantly, is it polite to do so? Modern urbanites may often ask themselves these questions. The answer is, much of the time, yes: In the close quarters provided by supermarket lines, DMV lines, movie-theater lines, nightclubs, and so on, it is not improper to attempt to strike up a conversation with another, lovely-to-look-at, person. Hitting on someone, if it starts as *polite conver-*

sation, is not rude. Polite conversation is, by definition, relatively impersonal, respectfully pleasant, and not-at-all lascivious. It is where all conversations with strangers should start. Sometimes it leads to deeper things. Sometimes it does not.

Polite people who are not interested in carrying on conversation understand that a bit of polite chitchat with strangers is unavoidable in a city, and will therefore give good-natured but blandly noncommittal answers before wishing the other person a good day and turning to their reading material (I carry something to read wherever I go).

Polite people who enjoy chatting with strangers will recognize less-than-enthusiastic responses and resume cheerful quiet.

If the conversation has been pleasant for both people, an end to it can sound like this:

"I've enjoyed talking with you. Would you like to talk again sometime? May I give you my card?"

"That would be very nice. Thank you."

or:

"I've enjoyed talking with you. Would you like to talk again sometime? May I give you my card?"

"I'm sorry I can't accept your offer, but it has been very nice talking to you."

Flirt and Get Hurt

**Dear
Social Grace,**

Last night at my kung fu class, I had the misfortune of having to work with this guy who was constantly cracking jokes, giggling, and coming out with stupid one-liners. Earlier in the class, we had all worked with other people, and I didn't hear any giggles then, so I know he was treating me differently because I'm a woman. I was too astonished to come up with a way to stop it there and then, so I spent the class trying to avoid reacting to his asinine behavior. It really pissed me off that I had to put up with this kind of energy.

There aren't so many of us that I can avoid this person in future classes. I've been practicing on my own saying, "You wouldn't say that to the boys, so don't say it to me. It's inappropriate."

My question is in the framework of a martial arts class, but it could apply to any situation. What line can a nonconfrontational woman use to immediately (but politely) put a stop to unwanted attention? I am so bad at immediate responses that I do have to practice. I think the built-in programming we have all received since girlhood to "be nice" is a handicap.

**Dear
Martial-Arts
Madam,**

In your martial arts class, the best response to a flirt would be something like "I'm sorry, but I'm here to improve my martial arts skills, and I need to concentrate." Or perhaps: "I need to focus on what we're learning; this really isn't an appropriate time to socialize." With the right mix of sternness and seriousness, you can get your point across.

The answer you've come up with seems to assume too much about the fellow's motives—and to be, perhaps, a bit harsher than is warranted. Sure, the poor guy may be dreaming of someday falling in love with a nice, old-fashioned gal with potent self-defense skills. You're not the woman for him, obviously, but it doesn't sound as though he's done anything all that horrible to you. Instead of telling him that he's "inappropriate," give him a chance to be the kung fu partner you'd like to work with. You'll both feel better about the situation.

And being nice isn't a bad thing. Many people could use a bit more "niceness programming," if you ask me. In social situations, blocking a flirtatious pass should have an element of kindness—a touch of "No, but thanks." Only if a flirt *then* refuses to leave you in peace or becomes aggressive should you resort to sterner measures—such as kung fu, in extreme cases.

If you are asked out by someone you don't want to spend time with, there are few things to keep in mind as you let that person down gently:

■ Don't say yes if you *really* want to say no (but keep in mind that romance can blossom in very unlikely places). It's not nice to waste another person's time. You should at least give him the option of thinking, "If only she'd gotten to know the real me. . . ."

- Don't beat around the bush. Saying that you are busy will only encourage her to ask you again. An acknowledgement of her thoughtful invitation and a polite "no thank you" are all that is required.

- Don't halt friendly relations. Avoiding eye contact with him the next time you are in the elevator together is unnecessary. You have every reason and obligation to treat unsuccessful suitors politely.

When two people agree to go on a date, they have entered into a social contract. This contract holds them responsible for some very basic good behavior—at least the same behavior you would expect to display on your first day at a new job: You show up appropriately dressed, appropriately clean, and behaving like a grown up.

On a first date, the "asker" traditionally pays for the evening— unless other arrangements are plainly understood beforehand—regardless of the genders of those involved. (It's nice—and not incorrect—for the "askee" to pop for a drink after dinner, say, or the popcorn at the movie.) Knowing who will be paying for what just makes things simpler when the check arrives. A considerate asker can even make his intentions plain when he extends his invitation, by using a phrase such as "I'd like to take you to dinner," for example.

It's also fine to ask someone out on a date while making it clear that you want to split costs; however, you might agree with me that such behavior is not exactly guaranteed to impress and should perhaps be saved until a relationship is floating along nicely. Then, saying something like "I could buy you dinner at Burrito Palace or we could split the cost of dinner at Chez Bissac" is a good approach.

The days when a woman might feel embarrassed about paying for her own meal are fast disappearing (and thank goodness). Yet there are circles in which a gentleman always pays for a lady. If both parties find this setup agreeable, then there are no worries. The problem comes when the people involved do not know whether they are *in* such a circle. If a lady invites a gentleman out to dine, for example, she should, to be fair, at least offer to pay. If the gentleman gently protests, she can either accept graciously, offer to split the check, or insist on paying herself (if she truly doesn't want to revolve in this "the gentleman always pays" orbit). The good news is that this is an early compatibility test. The better news is that as a relationship develops, agreements about this kind of thing are generally reached fairly quickly.

A polite person does not protest too much: If another person insists on buying your dinner, and your conscience and good sense will let you allow it, you should protest no more than twice before acquiescing. (Making a huge fuss over a restaurant bill is rather unseemly.)

Before you go on a date, mentally prepare for the worst. At least one of your carefully laid plans is certain to go horribly, horribly wrong. Be prepared to laugh it off. This is supposed to be fun. Besides, you can learn a lot about someone when plans go awry. (Keeping your cool makes a very good impression.) A smart person prepares for the best, too: Clean your apartment. Have coffee or the makings for after-dinner drinks. Wash your sheets. Have orange juice, bagels, and cream cheese in the refrigerator. For tomorrow—just in case.

On a date, your goal should be to talk no more than forty percent of the time. If silence erupts, don't panic—a little bit of quiet time is okay. If your date is not saying much, you can try to draw him out by asking questions, but try not to turn your conversation into an interview (avoid yes/no questions). Keep the conversation light and entertaining; save stories of childhood trauma for a

In the Cards

Single folks who are actively searching for romance might consider having some simple, business-size personal cards made, with their names and as much contact information as they feel comfortable giving to relative strangers. That way, they will not have to give out business cards (which contain information they may not want to give to every Tom, Dick, and Harriet they chat up on the subway), and they never have to worry about finding pens and pieces of paper. These cards are handy not only for single folks but also for others who may have need of a modern-day calling card. (True calling cards have fallen quite completely out of fashion; most modern urbanites will never see one.)

later date. And even though it is wise to date widely and often when you are searching for a soul mate, discussing other romances (or horrible past dating experiences) is poor form when you are speaking to someone you don't know very well. Many people have come to believe, often through exposure to too many reality-TV shows, that complete honesty and explicit openness are always good things. This is not true. (If someone throws a chair at you on national television, you have been perhaps *too* honest and open.) First, discussing other dates would seem to invite comparison, an obvious no-no. Second, going on about other dates can seem, if not unpleasantly boastful, deliberately insulting.

Having some preplanned conversational topics is a great confidence builder, and it can help keep you from stumbling into rough conversational terrain. In case you truly cannot think of anything to talk about, here is a list of 26 interesting and mostly uncontroversial topics of conversation for your reference: astronomy, bicycling, calligraphy, deep-sea diving, engineering, Fellini, ginseng, Henry VIII, insurance, juice bars, klezmer music, libraries, musical theater, number theory, olive trees, Paris, quilting, Roman ruins, style, the Treaty of Versailles, Underdog, vineyards, waterfalls, xylophagous insects, yoga, zeppelins. Feel free to use the alphabet to create your own list before you go out for an evening.

 Clever Kissing

Dear
Social Grace,

It's been a while since I've been in the "dating pool," and I have a couple of questions about proper "date" behavior. Is a kiss at the end of a first date too forward? I want to be proper and impress my date.

Dear Proper Madam or Sir,
Well, 100 Victorian poets agree that unconsummated desire is much more intense than the immediately satisfied kind, but ultimately, the decision of when to kiss is yours and your date's to make together. (And the official Social Grace biographers remind me that I would be, at best, a hypocrite if I were to call a first-date kiss improper.) Etiquette asks that third parties try not to pay too much attention to the tender, romantic happenings on others' doorsteps. At any rate, when it's time, you'll know. And it's always polite to ask.

The decision to have sex on a first date or any subsequent date is, of course, yours to make together. But be aware that while sex is a recreational activity for some, it is a binding contractual agreement for others. Both attitudes are just dandy, but when they clash, hurt feelings can result. This is only one reason it might be better to wait until you know each other better.

But sexual activity and etiquette are not mutually exclusive. You don't stop treating a person with respect just because you've seen him naked. The idea that etiquette and sex were not compatible has led to some pretty atrocious behavior by people who have decided that if sex is present then manners can go out the door. It is important to realize that etiquette has a very important place here, too. (And in fact, if you have set out to be a cheap tart, good manners will certainly smooth your path for you.)

Your etiquette obligations do not end when a date is over. What do you do when someone makes an effort to give you a pleasant evening, either by buying you dinner or just showing up all combed, shaved and perfumed? Well, a casual thank-you note makes a good impression. You could even send flowers if the occasion warranted it—but never send flowers (or, worse, balloons) to someone's workplace unless you know the recipient very well. And it is okay to call—the phone is not a toy, and it should not be used for playing elaborate mating-ritual games. There is no such thing as a "wait two days" rule. If you want to talk, call him. If your date doesn't want to talk, you can thank him for the evening and end the call.

If you can, date widely and often, and do not expect exclusivity until both parties have agreed to it. Before there is a mutual agreement about exclusivity, a person can and should date more than one person at a time. Standard dating practices in modern Western culture allow us to date whom we choose, until such time as all parties involved decide that they will pursue a relationship to the exclusion of others. Comparison-shopping just makes good sense. If no one has made any pledges of devotion yet, both parties should know (and accept) that on evenings when the other is "busy," "busy" may mean "eating sushi with someone else."

Online Romance

Dear
Social Grace,

If you join an online dating service, do you have to send replies to everyone who answers your ad, even if you're not interested in meeting them? I know it seems like the polite thing to do, but there are some other factors, such as: responses from guys who are kind of creepy, and sometimes too many responses to answer. What would you do?

Dear
Online Madam,

Yes, answering invitations (especially invitations you have, in a way, solicited) seems like the polite thing to do—because it *is* the polite thing to do. In our offline lives, we may receive romantic overtures from people who are not to our tastes, and we must gently rebuff them. The anonymity afforded by the Internet is a bad, not to mention cowardly, excuse for thoughtlessness. It would take but a few clicks to copy, paste, and send a simple "I'm terribly sorry, but I don't think we are compatible; good luck to you, though" form e-mail—you could answer hundreds of e-mail messages in minutes this way. Such a response is a basic act of courtesy, acknowledging that even online beaux have feelings. It's true that with online dating, the *need* for a "no thank you" seems to be obviated. All one has to deal with is an e-mail message, which by its nature is intangible and easily discarded. But those messages do represent actual, three-dimensional suitors—hopeful grins, sweaty palms, wilting bouquets, and all—and ignoring them seems wrong. Plus, you never know when or how rejected suitors are going to turn up in your life. Being thoughtless when dealing with strangers is just unwise.

We can also apply a three-dimensional-world rule to "creepy" e-mails, if by that term you mean inappropriate or downright frightening. They are best ignored—or reported to the authorities (in this case, the online-dating service) if necessary. But if you have inspired the beginnings of hopeful romantic feelings in the heart of a suitor who has no chance of winning your heart, try for a magnanimous gentleness when you send him on his way.

Bad dates happen to good people. Not every date ends in a long-term relationship—but this simple fact of life should not be the cause of any bad feelings whatsoever. Handled well, the date that does not end in love can lead to friendship, to a professional contact—even to a date with someone else.

When you get to the end of a bad date, find something nice to say. Something about the date must have been noteworthy. Was the movie's cinematography especially beautiful? Was the restaurant exceptionally clean? Try to say something positive about the evening, and say thank-you. But please do not say that you will be telephoning later if you will not be.

Excessively romantic public displays of affection are inconsiderate of others and often quite unpleasant to see—not to mention terribly juvenile. What you two do together is really none of our business, so try not to make it so. However, even Great Aunt Vivian cannot find fault with a couple who chastely holds hands.

Let's Give this Couple a Hand

Dear
Social Grace,

What are the etiquette rules around handholding between consenting adults? My honey and I like to hold hands. Is it impolite to do so in public? What about when socializing with other people? Does it make a difference if they are single people or couples? Does it matter if we are out walking, or sitting on the couch at someone's house, or holding hands under the table at dinner? We don't hold hands continually but have done so in all the aforementioned instances. I would like to know the etiquette rules on this issue.

Dear
Affectionate
Madam or Sir,

I hope to ease your mind about this handholding issue. And I sincerely hope that you haven't been withholding hand from your honey in anticipation of my answer to your question. And here it is: Holding hands is one of society's sanctioned ways of showing affection publicly, and it is available to everyone in most situations.

But, of course, handholding on escalators should be avoided. Many people are frustrated by couples who insist on holding hands while standing side by side on escalators, because this blocks those who want to pass on the left-hand side. By the same token, maybe holding hands on narrow sidewalks is impractical and obstructive. And holding hands in extremely formal situations (a state funeral, say) or while working at your job might seem rather odd. Other than in situations such as these, though, we need not put any restrictions on holding hands (accompanied only occasionally by ravenous looks of passionate longing, which can leave bystanders feeling mildly unsettled).

A thank-you note or call unaccompanied by a "Let's do it again" is a thoughtful way to end a non-starting relationship. Most people understand that not every coffee date or online exchange leads to a serious relationship, but having the tender shoots of romantic feeling brutally pruned can hurt. Rejection—even from someone we would have rejected first, given the chance—can bruise the ego. Don't just disappear without a word of farewell. If you are asked out again by a person you do not wish to see, the politest thing you can do is decline, with thanks. There is nothing inherently rude about saying no.

Ladies and Gentlemen

There is more difference within the sexes than between them.
—IVY COMPTON-BURNETT

In general, etiquette requires that we treat all people in a courteous way, without regard to race, religion, creed, and so on. Women and men, too, are to be treated with equal measures of respect; however, etiquette does allow for some distinctions between the sexes, when it comes to what I will call, for the sake of convenience, "ladies-first behavior." We as a society are still working out some of the social differences between men and women—thank goodness, we have weeded out many blatantly misogynist practices. We are left, to the delight of many people, with some traditional ladies-first behavior. Ladies-first behavior is often inappropriate nowadays—for example, it is improper in almost any work environment.

Many ladies do not enjoy it (and if that is a gal's preference, a true gentleman abides by it). Ladies, if you prefer that a gentleman not exhibit this sort of courtly behavior, you may simply tell him so, politely (for example, "Please don't stand up; it isn't necessary"). But there is no reason to be insulted right away—many thoroughly modern and liberated gentlemen were, for better or worse, raised to behave this way toward ladies, and they fall back on it out of habit.

And gentlemen, you might one day interact with people for whom ladies-first behavior is expected. They might not recognize your eschewing it as a feminist statement; indeed, they might think you something of a clod. Do with the knowledge what you will.

There are many social circles in which ladies-first behavior is the norm. An informal poll of some modern, independent females of my acquaintance reveals that many still like it—and expect it—in certain situations. So, gentlemen, if you are unsure whether it is appropriate, for instance, to hold doors for a lady you are getting to know, you are probably wise to err on the side of old-fashioned gentlemanly manners. And that's the first bit of etiquette we will discuss in this chapter.

In a social situation, it is still widely considered correct for a gentleman to stand when a lady approaches him (at a restaurant table, say), to hold doors for her, and so on. Rules like this are not always obvious to modern people who loll comfortably in the very casual atmosphere of the modern city, but they are good to keep in mind: This kind of conduct can earn a future mother-in-law's approval and goodwill almost immediately.

For people who might worry that this behavior is sexist, I will add that holding doors and standing when approached are just as easily applied to *everyone,* regardless of the genders

Congratulations?

Historically, congratulating brides-to-be was considered improper. While we might have congratulated a man on his good fortune in having the woman of his dreams consent to his marriage proposal, we didn't like to imply—by congratulating a woman—that she had succeeded in her endeavor to "catch" a husband. In the past, the "voracious, husband-hunting female" was a more common derogatory stereotype of women, and previous generations were therefore more sensitive to phrases that might allude to it. The rule seems rather old-fashioned nowadays, and I am not going to send anyone to Social Grace Detention for expressing warm wishes to nice people on happy occasions. Fortunately, it is no longer widely assumed that all women are on the lookout for eligible men to entrap in wedlock. Nonetheless, I suggest simply wishing newlyweds and newly engaged couples every happiness ("I'm so happy for you both") and *mazel tov*.

of the people involved, thereby extending courtly, respectful behavior to everyone instead of withholding it from everyone. Standing for any friend or acquaintance who approaches your dinner table is not incorrect. As we move toward not making any gender distinctions whatsoever, why not tread everyone with elegant respect, rather than with lazy disregard?

Both men and women rise when greeting guests, and both should rise when meeting someone much older, someone they especially admire, or even someone they have been looking forward to seeing. But tradition is tradition, and because it has long been customary for a woman to stay seated when introduced socially to a peer (male or female), there are some circles in which a woman's jumping up to shake hands (with another woman a few years older—Great Aunt Vivian, say) might even be taken as an insult (because of the "older" insinuation). When a gal finds herself in such old-fashioned circles, she generally knows it (the butler who answered the door should be a clue). Elsewhere, standing respectfully when meeting someone new is, regardless of your gender, a charming thing to do.

Ladies first. There are few exceptions to the ladies-first rule (revolving doors and doors that must be pushed open are important ones—a gentleman should enter first and do the pushing), so if you want to create an old-fashioned ladies-first atmosphere, you will seldom go wrong applying that rule when in doubt (again, we are speaking about social settings). At the theater, a man can follow a woman into a row (and take the aisle seat if he and his female companion are sitting at the end of a row). Nowadays, it is just as correct—and just as chivalrous—for a moviegoer of either sex to ask a companion which seat he or she prefers before sitting down.

Not too long ago, a lady out on the town with her fellow would have expected him to offer her his hand as an aid when she stepped out of a car, to help her out of her coat, and to carry her packages. These days, a man hoping to create a ladies-first atmosphere would be wise to perhaps preface any such action by asking permission ("May I take your coat?" for example). And again, this rule can be applied across genders—when one lady takes another to a romantic dinner, she might like to add a touch of chivalry to the evening this way. A lady can help a gentleman friend who is overburdened with packages. And so on.

The trick to making this work well is concerning yourself, first, with the comfort of the other people you are with.

 ## Riding in Cars with Ladies

Dear
Social Grace,

Say you are a gentleman on a date with a lady. You've had dinner, and you've reached your car and are preparing to head home. Because you are a gentleman, you unlock and open the car's passenger door for her and make sure she is seated inside. Now, I have two questions. Is it your job to also close the car door for her, or should she take care of that herself after she is situated?

Second, should she, to be polite, reach across and unlock your door for you (as it's raining and you fumble with your car keys)? Or is it considered more ladylike to just sit there and wait patiently for the gentleman to get into the car?

Dear
Gentlemanly Sir,

If you want to create an old-fashioned ladies-first atmosphere, the answer to both of your questions is clear: The lady should have as little contact with any door as possi-

Gays, Lesbians, Bisexuals, and Etiquette

Traditional etiquette did not have many rules in place for people whose romantic inclinations lay in the direction of their own genders; this led many to believe that such people were "outside the bounds" of proper social behavior. But that notion disregards etiquette's more fundamental directives: fairness, tolerance, and respect. If you are ever in doubt as to how to handle a situation with a gay person, those basic notions should be your guide.

For many years, etiquette split adults into two groups that were treated a bit differently: married people and unmarried people. The system's simplicity worked well. But these days, there are plenty of unmarried pairs—many of them, of course, gays and lesbians—who can and should be afforded treatment as "couples." Nowadays, it is perfectly proper to treat any "couple" as married if they are married in everything but name (if they own property together, have joint finances, or are raising children, they have earned at least that). One minor, illustrative example (but a very common problem, according to readers' questions) is addressing envelopes: The rule for a long time has been that married couples have their names together, joined by an *and*, on one line, while unmarried couple's names were stacked (without an *and*). Nowadays, any pair that is a social "couple" should be treated as such; roommates, for example, would get their names on separate lines (in the case of different last names, going by alphabetical order makes excellent sense in this situation and many others like it).

Language works in mysterious ways, and although some

other terms have been bandied about, *partner* is the ascendant appropriate term for a person's "spouse-equivalent." If you are unsure, you should fall back on that one. Otherwise, you should take your cue from the people involved. Note what term is used when the person is discussed or when an introduction is made—or if you are on friendly social terms, you may even ask what the people involved would like to be called.

❧ Curiosity about new types of people is normal, but it's never polite to ask new acquaintances directly about their sex lives. Generally speaking, when it becomes necessary for you to know what a person's preference is, you will find out naturally as you get to know each other.

ble. You open the car door for her, make sure all limbs and hems are safely inside before gently closing her door, and then open your door yourself.

The wording of your second paragraph suggests that you were perhaps a bit irritated by some lady, somewhere, who did not reach across and unlock your door while you struggled in the rain. Indeed, it's by no means incorrect for a passenger to unlock a driver's door after being let into a car; I'd even go so far as to call it a nice thing to do. If I've guessed correctly about your situation, the problem might have been that the lady in question thought she was on an old-fashioned, formal date, while you thought you had moved into informal territory. (It's generally a good idea to skew toward formal if you're unsure.) Or perhaps her skirt wouldn't allow her to lean gracefully across your gearshift. Whatever the reason, you mustn't hold it against her—she behaved properly. Most couples eventually do end up helping each other in and out of automobiles, so you probably won't spend the rest of your life unlocking both car doors.

I'll just add that modern dating etiquette takes into account that (gasp!) a lady may be the driver or that neither party might be a woman. Opening or unlocking a door for your date—regardless of your gender—is charming, courtly behavior that I heartily endorse.

If this chivalrous, mannerly treatment of others is going to catch on in a big way, we all have to employ it. Doesn't it make you feel good when someone holds a door for you, rather than letting it slam in your face after he (or she) walks through? Try to spread that happy feeling around. And if you see someone who, through his own kindness, is "trapped" holding a door while a horde of people pass through, offer to take over for him.

After You! No, After You!

As I enter Starbucks in the morning, often a man who approaches the door right in front of me will open the door for me and let me enter first because I am a woman. This lets me approach the line ahead of him, even though he was actually the first to arrive on the scene. So he ends up suffering for his act of chivalry. Is it more polite for me to wait after he opens the door so

214

that he can go ahead of me, or is going first in line another perk of the ladies-first policy here? I've tried to say, "After you," but that usually turns into both of us saying it back and forth, and it's all very difficult before a person has her morning latte.

Dear Morning Madam,

Let's pause and remember that we are talking about a matter of seconds: A person's wait in the latte line is affected only minimally by one person in front of him. That's not to say that "After you" isn't a lovely response to this polite gesture (and a behavior that I'd like to encourage not only at cafés but also at the bank, the DMV, and everywhere else people queue up). But if it is declined once, you need only offer thanks before proceeding to order your coffee drink.

Although romantic situations are often where ladies-first behavior is applied, romance is not the only situation where such behavior can be appropriate. For example, a gay man can and should offer to walk a woman friend to her car when she leaves a late party in an iffy part of town. A gentleman dining with his girlfriend and her best friend should make sure that they are both treated like ladies. And chivalrous behavior, for both men and women, looks an awful lot like the good manners we've discussed in preceding chapters: Treat others with respect, and keep your mind on their comfort and happiness.

On the Move

*A journey of a thousand miles
starts from beneath one's feet.*
—LAO TZU

We enjoy traveling because it exposes us to new people and places—but we must remember that traveling also exposes new people and places to us. The anonymity that travel affords us is no excuse for bad behavior, especially when we travel abroad. The "American" occupies a unique place in the consciousness of much of the world's population, and the reputation that precedes us on our travels is not necessarily a good one. Like many bad reputations, this one is based largely on misinformation.

When we travel to foreign countries, we have an opportunity to show off the American personality's better aspects, which include genuine friendliness and deep respect for other cultures. You can do your part to improve foreign relations (and increase your enjoyment of your trip) by following a few simple rules of courtesy. Before my first steps on foreign soil—in Canada, at the age of eleven—my father had a very serious talk with me about how my behavior in a foreign country reflected on every American. He was absolutely right, and I wish he could give that talk to every American traveler. I shall do my best to summarize its elements in this chapter.

Remember that every American is an American ambassador. Approach new places and customs with an open mind. (Really, if you can't do that, you are much better off staying home.) Try not to stare at people, especially when they are privately practicing religious or traditional rituals. And remember that no one likes to hear his country disparaged; even if a local makes deprecating remarks about his country, you should never respond with similar comments. Always be careful about comparing one country with another (even if it is a favorable comparison), and never make disapproving comments about the people and things you are seeing. You may feel protected by the fact that no one around you speaks English, but the moment you opine, "Isn't that the most hideous landscape you've ever seen?" you can be sure that the local English teacher will be standing behind you.

Many modern urbanites will be tempted, in an effort to fit in or to prove their worldliness, to make their own disparaging comments about the United States. But beware of straying from thoughtful discussions about politics and society, which can be very enjoyable parts of an overseas trip, into outright abuse, which is always offensive. It is shameful to allow your country, or any country, to be broadly defamed.

Some things were meant to be remembered, not photographed. Before taking a photograph of the local citizens, ask permis-

Traveling Companions

If you want to get along with your traveling companions, you have to plan ahead. One of the best ways to maintain peace with a friend or a significant other on a vacation is to make some detailed plans before you leave. This helps you avoid much of the weary bickering that can easily escalate into a serious argument when two people have been together, nonstop, for several days. And consider setting aside some private time, too—if you're dying to visit a certain museum and your traveling companion must visit a certain store, split up for an afternoon. (This will have the added bonus of giving you something to talk about over dinner.) Also make sure you have planned your budget—including incidentals such as food and souvenirs.

sion. (Of course, very large crowds are excepted.) Snapping photos of ordinary people (even though they may look extraordinary to you) going about their daily business is a definite no-no.

You should learn a few phrases in the language of any foreign country you visit. We are very fortunate that much of the world's population speaks at least a bit of English, but courtesy requires that a guest in a foreign country be able to say a few words in that country's tongue. You should be able to muddle through a good portion of the following words and phrases: "please," "thank you," "excuse me," "good morning/afternoon/evening," "yes," "no," "good," "beautiful," and "I'm sorry, I don't speak _____." (Add phrases such as "Where is the flea market?" as you will.)

Remember that when you encounter a language-based communication problem, shouting is not helpful. Try to keep your voice conversational, and if you are traveling in an area where you do not speak the language and where English is not widely spoken, carry a small phrasebook with you. You may resist this idea because it will make you look like a tourist. But you *are* a tourist (there is no shame in that)—and anyway, the only people you might fool into thinking that you are anything else would be other tourists.

Similarly, one should make an effort to learn the local customs of the places one visits. This is not a very difficult undertaking if your destination is, say, Denver. But a trip to Rome really does require that we understand a little bit about "what the Romans do." You should have a guidebook before you leave the United States. On the plane, you can start acclimating yourself to your destination by doing some quick, painless research. Make note of important taboos, tipping guidelines, typical dining habits, and so on.

Pack light (and suitably for your accommodations). My Great Aunt Vivian has given me much practical advice over the years, and I can share this bit with you: Never pack more than you can carry for a mile, up a hill, in the rain—because you might have to do just that. Your luggage should be compact, neat, and labeled, and if it is too big to be lifted into an overhead bin, it is too big to be brought into a plane's cabin. Check it. There is nothing more irritating than a passenger who inconveniences people so that his luggage may have special treatment.

An airplane, train, or bus is a public place. You are not invisible just because you are surrounded by foreigners who do not speak your language. And rules of proper behavior are not put on hold just because you're suspended thousands of feet above the earth. An airplane seat is not the place for clipping your toenails. Since space on an airplane is so limited, in fact, you need to be even more courteous than usual.

 ## No Rest for the Elbows

Dear Social Grace,

I have an argument for you to settle: Is there a rule about who gets the armrest of an airplane seat? Although this is a playful debate between me and a friend, and it's a joking argument about whose armrest was whose during a recent flight, I'm genuinely curious (although I usually just give up my armrest rather than make an issue of it).

Dear Strong-Armed Madam or Sir,

It's helpful to think of armrests as barriers that keep us from elbowing each other in the ribs. No one has a "right" to them. Friends should be able to come up with an amicable agreement about sharing a dividing armrest—his elbow in front, yours in back, for example—but I'm sure you know that. If you are genuinely uncomfortable in your seat and the armrest is occupied, it is not impolite to ask the person sitting next to you if you might share.

Ugly Americans

*Dear
Social Grace,*

Recently, I was out to dinner with some colleagues during a conference in a foreign country. Also joining us was "Marlena," a local woman who had been our tour guide and who had become a friend to me during the weeklong meeting. I had wanted to take Marlena out to dinner to thank her for her hospitality; however, when the bill came, one of my colleagues, "Norman," did not handle the situation tactfully. Norman picked up the check with a statement directed at Marlena that showed disdain for her country's economic situation: "I make more money in one day than you do in a week." Our guest was visibly dismayed. Norman then added insult to injury by disregarding the local gratuity practices and insisted on leaving a twenty percent tip because "that's the way we do it in America." I was uncertain of how to apologize to Marlena for his actions, and I certainly did not want her to associate me with this attitude toward her country. What should I have said to Marlena?

Dear American
Madam or Sir,

There are ugly Americans, who don't care that they cause offense, and there are stupid Americans, who don't see why implying that a person's country is backward and her financial situation embarrassing would be insulting. There are also ugly *and* stupid Americans—the hardest to deal with, because they not only don't know how to behave but also don't care to learn.

Apologizing for another person's actions isn't necessary in every situation. But in this one, since both you and your colleague represent not only your country but also your organization, some expression of regret on your part would have been in order. In your place, I might have given Norman the chance to prove himself merely stupid (rather than ugly) and to apologize for himself by saying, "I don't think you said what you meant to say, Norman. Marlena, I'm so sorry." If Norman persisted in being a boor, I would have tried to change the subject and then apologized to Marlena later, privately, on behalf of the group I represented. Pressing the point might only have antagonized Norman and embarrassed Marlena further.

You will not be able to adapt to every custom in the foreign lands you visit. If you try, you will not have time to enjoy your holidays. Everyone must make allowances for foreign visitors, who cannot (and should not be expected to) learn all the social requirements of the places they visit only briefly. After you have learned what you can about local customs, apply that knowledge to a sturdy base of good old-fashioned American etiquette. Together, they will see you around the world, and safely, courteously, back home.

Further Reading

In writing the Social Grace etiquette column, I often refer to the following books, and I recommend them all as excellent resources for further reading. (And please look for other books by these esteemed authors.)

Baldridge, Letitia. *Complete Guide to the New Manners for the '90s.* New York: Macmillan Publishing Company, 1990.

Carter, Stephen L. *Civility.* New York: Harper Perennial, 1998.

Condé Nast Publications. *Vogue's Book of Etiquette.* New York: Condé Nast Publications, 1969.

Corinth, Kay, and Sargent, Mary. *All About Entertaining.* New York: David McKay Company, 1966.

Eichler, Lillian. *The New Book of Etiquette.* Garden City, New York: Garden City Publishing, 1924.

Martin, Judith. *Miss Manners Rescues Civilization.* New York: Crown Publishers, 1996.

Mercedes, Mary. *A Book of Courtesy.* San Francisco: HarperSanFrancisco, 2001.

Post, Emily. *Etiquette.* New York: Funk & Wagnalls Company, 1940.

Post, Peggy. *Emily Post's Entertaining.* New York: HarperPerennial, 1998.

Post, Peggy. *Emily Post's Etiquette,* sixteenth edition. New York: Harper Collins, 1997.

Roosevelt, Eleanor. *Eleanor Roosevelt's Book of Common Sense Etiquette.* New York: Macmillan Publishing Company, 1962.

Vanderbilt, Amy. *Amy Vanderbilt's Complete Book of Etiquette.* New York: Doubleday and Company, 1952.

Visser, Margaret. *The Rituals of Dinner.* New York: Penguin Books, 1991.

227